Sunset
Cooking for Two

By the Editors of Sunset Books and Sunset Magazine

Sunset Publishing Corporation ■ *Menlo Park, California*

Casual dining for two couldn't be better than this! Serve Grilled Turkey on Sesame Buns (recipe on page 51) with red peppers in Herb Vinaigrette (recipe on page 44).

*S*et a Table for Two

What's the occasion? Whether you're planning a weekend patio picnic or an evening of roses and romance, this book offers you just the recipes you're looking for—and every one of them is designed to serve just two.

You'll find a full calendar of menu ideas for any time of day or year, from brandy-spiked breakfast French toast to hearty luncheon salads to elegantly sauced lobster and scallops for a celebration dinner. And throughout the book, you'll discover ways to enjoy classic dishes you never expected to cook in small quantity.

Whether you're just starting out together or you've been partners for years, let the delicious contents of this cook book make each of your meals for two a very special event.

A heartfelt thank you to Laurin Lynch and Dave Puntel for their valuable assistance with the photographs, and to Fillamento, Beaver Bros. Antiques, and Cottonwood for their generosity in sharing props for use in our photographs. Thanks also to Rebecca LaBrum for editing the manuscript and to Viki Marugg for her creative contributions to the artwork.

For our recipes, we provide a nutritional analysis (see page 5) prepared by Hill Nutrition Associates, Inc., of Florida.

Research & Text
Tori Ritchie Bunting

Coordinating Editor
Linda J. Selden

Design
Sandra Popovich

Illustrations
Nobu Kaji

Photographers: **Kevin Sanchez:** *2, 7, 10, 15, 18, 23, 26, 31, 34, 39, 42, 47, 50, 55, 58, 63, 66, 71, 74, 79, 82, 87, 90;* **Nikolay Zurek:** *95.*

Photo Stylist
Susan Massey-Weil

Calligraphy
Sherry Bringham

About the Recipes

All of the recipes in this book were tested and developed in the *Sunset* test kitchens.

Food and Entertaining Editor, Sunset Magazine
Jerry Anne Di Vecchio

Cover: Scallops & Lobster in Tomato Cream Sauce (recipe on page 89). Design by Susan Bryant. Photography by Kevin Sanchez. Photo styling by Susan Massey-Weil. Food styling by Tori Ritchie Bunting.

Editor, Sunset Books: Elizabeth L. Hogan

First printing September 1991

Contents

Just for Two

Sooner or later, there comes a time when you'll be cooking for just two people. Perhaps you're searching out new dishes to woo somebody special. Or maybe you and your sweetheart are just starting out as a couple, and you need a repertoire of recipes for all occasions. Then again, you may be making the transition back to meals for two after a lifetime of cooking for a family. Whatever your circumstances, cooking for two requires a different approach than preparing meals for a crowd.

Most cook books focus on recipes yielding four to eight servings, leaving the two-person household with a never-ending stream of leftovers. But the dishes in this book are proportioned to serve only two, without waste. Though individual appetites do vary, we think you'll agree that our recipes usually offer just the amount of food you need.

While dinner may occupy most of your kitchen time, *Cooking for Two* also provides delicious breakfast and brunch selections, easy desserts and sweet snacks, and plenty of savory solutions for lunch. All in all, you'll find over 100 recipes to choose from, for any time of day.

Besides practical ideas for everyday meals, we've included a special section of "Candlelight Classics": perfectly planned menus for intimate occasions. These romantic, festive ideas for anniversaries, Valentine's Day, wintry fireside suppers, and summer sunset picnics will surely inspire you to create an unforgettable meal—and the beautiful photographs accompanying the menus will provide suggestions for table settings.

Throughout the book, you'll also find a series of special features that offer basic recipes designed to add interest and flavor to any meal. On page 44, for example, we suggest four ways to jazz up two ever-popular side dishes—plain bread and green salad. Another feature (see page 53) offers a selection of lowfat, salt-free homemade condiments; use these in endless ways on meats, fish, poultry, and vegetables. If you own a microwave, you'll learn how it can help you prepare satisfying, nutritious grain dishes in a snap (see page 69). Or look to page 76 for sweet sauces and syrups to create fuss-free desserts. With these features, you'll easily be able to turn a plain broiled chop, some tossed greens, and a bowl of sliced fresh fruit into a personalized, attractive meal.

Cooking for Two at Home

Though restaurant dinners and take-out food do offer convenient alternatives to home cooking for two, there's just no substitute for homemade meals. The food is fresher, it's seasoned exactly to your taste, and it can be every bit as convenient as purchased fare.

Whatever your timetable on a given day, you'll find choices in this book that fit into your plans. Many recipes can be prepared in about half an hour, such as tempting Curried Turkey & Broccoli (page 52) or elegant Asian-style Pasta Primavera (page 30). Other dishes are ideal for slower, lazier days when you can linger in the kitchen or perhaps share some time cooking together. The preparation and cooking times printed at the start of each recipe let you know in advance how well each dish suits your schedule.

In addition to convenience, nutrition is probably important to you. Each of our recipes is accompanied by a nutritional analysis that tells you at a glance what that dish contributes to your diet (see "About Our Nutritional Data" below). Again, there's plenty of variety; as easily as they mold to your time schedule, these recipes will fit your nutritional mood of the moment. Choose from lean dishes that limit fat; meatless recipes to help cut cholesterol; rich delights for well-earned splurges; and middle-of-the-road selections that neither deny nor indulge. (If you're particularly concerned about sodium intake, you may wish to substitute low- or reduced-sodium chicken broth and soy sauce for the regular-sodium products used in our recipes.)

A Kitchen for Two

Efficient cooking for two may mean re-evaluating your kitchen equipment. A few basic tools help scaled-down meals go together much more smoothly; fortunately, you probably already own many of these utensils. In testing the recipes for this book, we found the following equipment most helpful.

A *heavy-bottomed 1½- to 2-quart pan* with a tight-fitting lid is indispensable for cooking small-scale stews, soups, side dishes, and sauces. For toasting small quantities of nuts, a *small frying pan* (4- to 6-inch diameter) is the best choice. One all-purpose implement you'll use again and again is a good-quality *medium-size frying pan* (8- to 10-inch diameter); if you're trying to cut down on fat, you may want to buy one with a nonstick surface.

A *small glass soufflé dish* (about 1½-quart size) is handy for baked vegetable dishes, mini-casseroles, and egg stratas, and it doubles as an excellent storage container. *Small baking dishes*, such as a 7-by 11-inch rectangular or 1½- to 2-quart oval dish, are just right for holding two fish fillets, chicken pieces, or chops. *Scaled-down ramekins and gratin dishes*, sold in cookware stores in various patterns and sizes, provide a pretty presentation for individual portions.

If you like to cook outdoors, a *small barbecue* (about 14-inch diameter) is a great investment that you'll really have fun using. A *toaster oven* lets you bake or toast small amounts of food without the energy waste involved in heating a large oven. And of course, the *microwave oven* offers maximum convenience in many ways; we've designed some special grain dishes that take advantage of this kitchen savior (see page 69).

Shopping & Storage Tips

When shopping for two, always keep in mind the goal of avoiding waste and leftovers. Perfect the art of searching out smaller basic vegetables, such as onions (which run the gamut from nut-size to king-size), carrots, and potatoes. Remember that fresh produce is actually easier to control in terms of volume, since canned and frozen vegetables often are sold in amounts too great for most two-serving recipes. Remember, also, that fresh seasonal produce has exemplary flavor and nutritive value.

Of course, it makes sense to buy some foods in quantity—but if you do, you'll need to pay a little extra attention to storage. Consider shaping ground meat into patties and freezing them in well-wrapped bundles of two; store chops, chicken thighs, and chicken breast halves the same way. Nuts, bread, Parmesan and other hard cheeses, and sticks of butter all store well in airtight freezer wrapping. Leftover bread from a big baguette can be whirled in a food processor to make fine bread crumbs; pack these in airtight freezer bags and scoop out the amount you need, a little at a time.

If making homemade chicken broth appeals to you (and we highly recommend it as a means of cutting sodium), prepare and chill a large batch, then ladle 1-cup portions into airtight storage bags. Arrange on a baking sheet, freeze until firm, and store in the freezer to use as needed.

The Most Important Ingredient

Whether you're a pragmatist or a romantic (or a little of both), you'll find recipes for your lifestyle in the pages ahead; just browse through each chapter and select whatever suits you best. We hope our photographs will inspire you to set mealtime moods, from elegant to casual—from a lacy cloth and soft lighting to country-style platters on a patio table. But no matter what the presentation, the most important ingredient in cooking for two is the one that's always there: the two of you, spending a few moments together to share a meal.

About Our Nutritional Data

For our recipes, we provide a nutritional analysis stating calorie count; grams of protein, carbohydrates, and total fat; and milligrams of cholesterol and sodium. Generally, the analysis applies to a single serving, based on the number of servings given for each recipe and the amount of each ingredient. If a range is given for the number of servings and/or the amount of an ingredient, the analysis is based on an average of the figures given.

The nutritional analysis does not include optional ingredients or those for which no specific amount is stated. If an ingredient is listed with a substitution, the information was calculated using the first choice.

Eye Openers

Pictured on facing page

Brandied French Toast

Preparation time: About 20 minutes

Cooking time: About 7 minutes

Bring the feeling of a bed and breakfast inn to your home with this rich, fragrantly spiced specialty. To complete the meal, offer fresh-squeezed orange juice and papaya slices with berries; serve mugs of steaming coffee or tea alongside the French toast. And dress up the table with a big bouquet of sunny fresh flowers!

   4 slices coarse-textured sourdough French bread, *each* **about 4 inches wide, 5 inches long, and ¾ inch thick**

   2 eggs

  ¼ cup half-and-half
     Maple syrup

   1 tablespoon orange juice

   1 tablespoon brandy (or 1 tablespoon more orange juice)

  ¼ teaspoon ground cinnamon

  ⅛ teaspoon ground nutmeg
     Orange Butter (recipe follows)
     Melted butter or margarine
     Powdered sugar
     Thin strips of orange peel (optional)

Select a dish large enough to hold bread in a single layer. In dish, beat together eggs, half-and-half, 1 tablespoon syrup, orange juice, brandy, cinnamon, and nutmeg; add bread and turn to coat. Let stand, turning bread once or twice, until liquid has been absorbed (about 5 minutes).

Meanwhile, prepare Orange Butter.

Heat an electric griddle to 375° (or place a wide frying pan over medium-high heat). Brush lightly with melted butter. Add bread and cook, turning once, until slices are golden brown on both sides and hot in center (about 7 minutes). Serve warm, with Orange Butter, powdered sugar, and maple syrup. Garnish with orange peel, if desired. Makes 2 servings.

Per serving without Orange Butter: 314 calories, 12 g protein, 38 g carbohydrates, 10 g total fat, 225 mg cholesterol, 381 mg sodium

Orange Butter. In a small bowl, beat ¼ cup **butter** or margarine (at room temperature) with 1 teaspoon grated **orange peel** and 1 tablespoon **orange-flavored liqueur** or orange juice until well blended. Makes 2 servings.

Per serving: 225 calories, 0.3 g protein, 3 g carbohydrates, 23 g total fat, 62 mg cholesterol, 234 mg sodium

You don't need to leave home to enjoy this bountiful
country-inn breakfast. Topped with syrup and a sweet orange-
flavored butter, thick slices of Brandied French Toast (recipe on facing page)
are a perfect start to a leisurely weekend. Serve with fresh fruit,
chilled orange juice, and plenty of hot coffee.

Hearty Healthy Hotcakes

Preparation time: About 10 minutes

Cooking time: About 1½ minutes

Making pancakes from scratch is easier than you might think—and these flavorful hotcakes, enriched with oats and cornmeal, offer further incentive to get out your mixing bowls. Try Apple & Sausage Sauté (page 12) alongside.

> ¼ cup *each* cornmeal, regular rolled oats, and all-purpose flour
> 1 tablespoon sugar
> ½ teaspoon baking powder
> ¼ teaspoon baking soda
> Pinch of salt
> 1 egg yolk
> ⅔ cup buttermilk
> 2 egg whites
> Salad oil

In a bowl, combine cornmeal, oats, flour, sugar, baking powder, baking soda, and salt. In another bowl, whisk egg yolk and buttermilk to blend. Pour buttermilk mixture into dry ingredients; stir just until evenly moistened.

In a clean, dry bowl, beat egg whites with an electric mixer on high speed until they hold soft peaks. Gently fold whites into batter.

Heat an electric griddle to 375° (or place a wide frying pan over medium-high heat). Brush griddle lightly with oil.

For each pancake, spoon about ⅓ cup of the batter onto griddle. Cook until pancakes are bubbly on top and medium brown on bottom (about 1 minute). Turn pancakes over and cook until medium brown on other side (about 30 more seconds). Makes 2 servings (about 3 pancakes *each*).

Per serving: 283 calories, 12 g protein, 43 g carbohydrates, 7 g total fat, 110 mg cholesterol, 419 mg sodium

Mini Tomato-Olive Stratas

Preparation time: About 15 minutes

Chilling time: At least 4 hours

Baking time: About 35 minutes

Layers of bread, cheese, and vegetables baked in an egg custard compose the one-dish meal called a *strata*. These individual stratas, assembled in small au gratin or soufflé dishes, feature ripe olives, jack cheese, and both fresh and dried tomatoes. To complete a substantial breakfast or brunch, simply add your choice of juice and fresh fruit.

> 6 slices firm-textured white or oatmeal bread, *each* about 4 by 5 inches
> 1 cup (about 4 oz.) shredded jack cheese
> 2 small pear-shaped tomatoes, thinly sliced
> 2 tablespoons drained, minced dried tomatoes packed in oil
> 1 can (about 2¼ oz.) sliced ripe olives, drained
> 3 eggs
> ¾ cup milk
> ½ teaspoon pepper

Butter two 4- by 7-inch au gratin dishes (at least 2 inches deep) or two 1-quart soufflé dishes. Cut bread slices in half diagonally to make 12 triangles.

In bottom of each buttered dish, place 3 bread triangles, overlapping slightly if necessary. Sprinkle a fourth of the cheese over bread in each dish. Layer sliced tomatoes, minced dried tomatoes, and olives on top of cheese, dividing equally between dishes. Then cover each strata with 3 more bread triangles and sprinkle each with half the remaining cheese.

In a bowl, beat eggs and milk to blend. Pour half the mixture into each dish, moistening entire surface; sprinkle with pepper. Cover with plastic wrap and refrigerate for at least 4 hours or until next day, pressing stratas once or twice with a fork to help bread absorb liquid completely.

Remove dishes from refrigerator, uncover, and transfer directly to a cold oven; then turn on oven to 350°. Bake stratas until golden brown and bubbly (about 35 minutes). Let cool for 10 minutes, then serve. Makes 2 servings.

Per serving: 728 calories, 34 g protein, 52 g carbohydrates, 44 g total fat, 392 mg cholesterol, 1,647 mg sodium

Rolled Corn Frittata

Preparation time: About 15 minutes

Cooking time: About 10 minutes

A *frittata* is a hearty Italian-style omelet, made by cooking eggs together with fresh vegetables and seasonings. This frittata, plump with corn kernels and bell pepper chunks, can be served unadorned or, for a Latin accent, topped with sour cream and salsa. Home fries and hot corn muffins with honey are perfect companions.

  1   tablespoon butter or margarine
  ¾   cup fresh corn kernels; or ¾ cup frozen corn kernels, thawed
  1   small red or green bell pepper, seeded and diced
  ⅓   cup thinly sliced green onions
  3   eggs
  2   tablespoons half-and-half or milk
  ⅛   teaspoon liquid hot pepper seasoning
       Salt
       Sour cream and purchased salsa (optional)

Melt butter in a medium-size nonstick frying pan over medium heat. Add corn and bell pepper and cook, stirring often, until pepper is just tender to bite (about 5 minutes). Add onions and cook, stirring often, until limp (about 1 minute).

In a bowl, whisk together eggs, half-and-half, and hot pepper seasoning. Pour over vegetables in pan; quickly tilt pan to distribute egg mixture evenly. Cook, lifting edges with a spatula to let uncooked portion flow underneath, until frittata is set but still moist on top (about 4 minutes). Tilt pan and roll frittata out onto a plate; season to taste with salt. Cut frittata in half and transfer to warm plates. Spoon sour cream and salsa over each portion, if desired. Makes 2 servings.

Per serving: 243 calories, 12 g protein, 15 g carbohydrates, 16 g total fat, 340 mg cholesterol, 178 mg sodium

Zucchini-Basil Omelet for Two

Preparation time: About 15 minutes

Cooking time: About 12 minutes

Streamline your omelet making by preparing a double recipe in one pan; to serve, just cut the omelet in half. Warm pita bread triangles and assorted fresh fruit nicely round out the meal.

  3   tablespoons butter or margarine
  2   medium-size zucchini, diced
       Coarsely ground pepper
  ¼   cup chopped fresh basil
  5   eggs
  2   tablespoons water
  ¾   cup shredded jack cheese
  ¼   cup canned crushed tomatoes

Melt 2 tablespoons of the butter in a 2- to 3-quart pan over medium-high heat. Add zucchini and cook, stirring often, just until tender-crisp to bite (about 3 minutes). Season to taste with pepper. Reduce heat, cover, and continue to cook until tender to bite (about 5 more minutes). Stir in basil and set aside.

In a bowl, lightly beat eggs and water to blend. Melt remaining 1 tablespoon butter in a wide nonstick frying pan over medium-high heat; tilt pan to coat bottom and sides. Pour in egg mixture and cook, lifting edges with a spatula to let uncooked portion flow underneath, until set but still moist on top (about 4 minutes). Sprinkle cheese over half of omelet, then top cheese with zucchini mixture and tomatoes. Remove from heat; tilt pan and slide omelet onto a platter, flipping untopped portion over filling. Cut omelet in half and transfer to warm plates. Makes 2 servings.

Per serving: 533 calories, 29 g protein, 9 g carbohydrates, 43 g total fat, 615 mg cholesterol, 616 mg sodium

Busy days often begin with a quick cup of black coffee—and a quicker dash out the door. But even when you're in a hurry, you can still enjoy Yogurt Sundaes with Cinnamon Breadsticks (recipe on facing page). Fresh strawberries, tart yogurt, whole almonds, and a touch of maple syrup add up to a nutritious breakfast that's so easy to assemble you'll have time to sit down with the morning paper.

Yogurt Sundaes with Cinnamon Breadsticks

Preparation time: About 15 minutes

Baking time: About 10 minutes

For a quick and nutritious breakfast, layer plain yogurt with nuts and fruit, then serve with giant-size "sticks" of cinnamon toast. To speed things up, you can bake the toast and nuts at the same time. Completing the meal is easy; just add fresh juice and hot coffee or tea.

        Cinnamon Breadsticks (recipe follows)
    ⅓   cup whole unblanched almonds or hazelnuts
    2   cups plain lowfat yogurt
    1½ cups hulled, halved strawberries
    2   to 3 tablespoons maple syrup

Prepare and bake Cinnamon Breadsticks. Also spread nuts in an 8- or 9-inch pie pan; bake in a 400° oven alongside breadsticks until lightly browned and fragrant (about 10 minutes), stirring occasionally. Let cool slightly.

In two 16-ounce bowls or glasses, layer yogurt, nuts, and strawberries; add syrup to each serving to taste. Serve with Cinnamon Breadsticks. Makes 2 servings.

Per serving without Cinnamon Breadsticks: 366 calories, 17 g protein, 44 g carbohydrates, 15 g total fat, 14 mg cholesterol, 165 mg sodium

Cinnamon Breadsticks. Cut 1 small **baguette** (about 4 oz.) lengthwise into quarters; place on a large baking sheet. Brush cut sides of bread with 2 tablespoons **butter** or margarine, melted. Mix 2 tablespoons **sugar** with ½ teaspoon **ground cinnamon;** sprinkle evenly over cut sides of bread. Bake in a 400° oven until toasted (about 10 minutes). Makes 2 servings.

Per serving: 316 calories, 5 g protein, 44 g carbohydrates, 13 g total fat, 33 mg cholesterol, 446 mg sodium

Apricot Jam Sticks with Poached Apricots

Preparation time: About 15 minutes

Cooking time: About 12 minutes

Here's a special but simple breakfast. Cream cheese and apricot jam bake to sweet goodness inside rolled flour tortillas; sunny spiced apricots are served alongside. You might also offer poached eggs and hot herb tea.

    2   flour tortillas, *each* about 7 inches in diameter
    1   small package (about 3 oz.) cream cheese
    ¼   cup apricot jam
    2   teaspoons milk
    1   teaspoon sugar
        Poached Apricots (recipe follows)

Cut each tortilla in half. Cut cream cheese into 4 portions; shape each portion into a log about 5 inches long. Place one cream cheese log and 1 tablespoon of the jam near cut edge of each tortilla half. Roll tortillas around cheese and jam to enclose; place, seam side down, in a 9-inch pie pan.

Brush rolls with milk, then sprinkle evenly with sugar.

Bake in a 450° oven until tortillas are golden (about 12 minutes). Remove immediately from pan to prevent sticking.

While jam sticks are baking, prepare Poached Apricots. Serve warm jam sticks with apricots alongside. Makes 2 servings.

Poached Apricots. Halve and pit 4 medium-size ripe **apricots;** place in a small pan and add ½ cup **water.** (Or use ¼ cup water and 1 small can—about 8½ oz.—apricot halves in extra-light syrup.) Stir in 1 tablespoon **sugar,** ½ teaspoon **whole cloves,** and 1 small **cinnamon stick.**

Bring to a boil over high heat, then reduce heat and simmer until fruit is heated through and slightly softened (about 10 minutes for fresh fruit, 5 minutes for canned). With a slotted spoon, transfer fruit to 2 small bowls; strain poaching liquid and spoon over fruit.

Per serving: 399 calories, 7 g protein, 58 g carbohydrates, 17 g total fat, 47 mg cholesterol, 275 mg sodium

Broiled Cheese & Fruit Plate

Preparation time: About 15 minutes

Broiling time: About 2 minutes

When the day dawns hot, avoid the usual breakfast entrées and serve this refreshingly cool salad—a simple combination of fruit, Brie cheese, and crisp lettuce. (Another time, you might choose the same dish for brunch or lunch.) Complement the salad with thinly sliced ham and individual brioches.

- 3 tablespoons salad oil
- 2 tablespoons raspberry or red wine vinegar
- 2 teaspoons honey
- 1 cup seedless grapes, rinsed
- 1 medium-size Asian or Bartlett pear, cored and thinly sliced
- 1 piece (about 4 oz.) firm-ripe Brie cheese, cut in half
- 4 cups bite-size pieces butter lettuce, rinsed and crisped

In a large bowl, mix oil, vinegar, and honey. Add grapes and pear; stir to coat.

Place cheese pieces slightly apart in an 8- or 9-inch pie pan. Brush cheese with about 1 tablespoon of the dressing from the fruit mixture. Broil about 4 inches below heat until cheese is warm and begins to melt around edges (about 2 minutes).

Add lettuce to fruit mixture. Mix well, then divide between 2 dinner plates. With a wide spatula, lift warm cheese from pan; place one piece on each salad. Makes 2 servings.

Per serving: 514 calories, 14 g protein, 36 g carbohydrates, 37 g total fat, 57 mg cholesterol, 364 mg sodium

Apple & Sausage Sauté

Preparation time: About 10 minutes

Cooking time: About 8 minutes

Take a break from plain sausage and try this tangy-sweet blend of meat and fruit. It's bound to become a favorite accompaniment for almost any breakfast dish—scrambled eggs, pancakes, French toast, or even just English muffins or toasted bagels.

- 2 mild Italian sausages (about 8 oz. *total*), cut into ½-inch-thick slices
- ¼ cup water
- 2 tablespoons lemon juice
- 1 tablespoon honey
- ¼ teaspoon *each* ground ginger, ground coriander, and curry powder
- 2 medium-size apples, cored and cut into ½-inch-thick slices

Place a medium-size frying pan over high heat; when pan is hot, add sausages. Cook, stirring constantly, until sausage slices are no longer pink in center; cut to test (about 5 minutes).

Spoon off and discard all but 1 tablespoon of the drippings from pan. Add water and bring to a boil. Push sausages to side of pan; stir lemon juice, honey, ginger, coriander, and curry powder into liquid in pan. Push sausages into spice mixture and stir to coat well; remove with a slotted spoon and keep warm.

Add apples to pan and reduce heat to medium-high. Cook, stirring, until fruit is glazed and lightly browned (about 3 minutes). Return sausages to pan and stir to combine; serve immediately. Makes 2 servings.

Per serving: 433 calories, 17 g protein, 32 g carbohydrates, 27 g total fat, 69 mg cholesterol, 801 mg sodium

Breakfast Trout Fry

Preparation time: *About 15 minutes*

Cooking time: *About 35 minutes*

For a hearty weekend brunch or campsite breakfast, try pan-fried trout flanked by golden brown potatoes. The tantalizing aroma alone is sure to wake up appetites. Serve with a pot of freshly brewed coffee and, perhaps, warm muffins.

- 3 slices bacon (about 3 oz. *total*), chopped
- 2 large red thin-skinned potatoes (*each* about 3 inches in diameter), scrubbed and thinly sliced
  Salad oil (if needed)
- 1 small onion, thinly sliced
- ½ teaspoon dry thyme
- 2 cleaned whole trout (8 to 10 oz. *each*)
  All-purpose flour
  Salt and pepper

Cook bacon in a wide frying pan over medium heat until crisp (about 5 minutes), stirring often. Lift out with a slotted spoon, drain, and set aside. Spoon off and reserve 2 tablespoons of the bacon drippings.

Add potatoes to drippings remaining in pan and cook until browned on bottom (about 10 minutes); if necessary, add oil to prevent sticking. Add onion and thyme; turn carefully with a wide spatula to mix with potatoes. Continue to cook, turning occasionally, until potatoes are golden brown all over and tender when pierced (about 15 more minutes). Stir in bacon, then spoon mixture onto a warm platter and keep warm.

While potatoes are cooking, rinse fish, pat dry, and dust lightly with flour.

When potatoes are done, heat reserved 2 tablespoons bacon drippings in pan; then add fish. Cook, turning once with a wide spatula, until fish are browned on outside and opaque but still moist inside; cut in thickest part to test (about 5 minutes). Serve fish with potatoes; season to taste with salt and pepper. Makes 2 servings.

Per serving: 520 calories, 34 g protein, 38 g carbohydrates, 25 g total fat, 92 mg cholesterol, 333 mg sodium

Grilled Ham & Pineapple Sandwiches

Preparation time: *About 10 minutes*

Cooking time: *About 5 minutes*

Break the rules and serve the unconventional for breakfast! Nothing could be more satisfying than this hot ham and cheese sandwich with a hint of sugar and spice, especially when it's served with a glass of cold milk and a melon wedge.

- 4 slices rye or whole wheat bread, *each* about 4 by 5 inches
  About 1 tablespoon butter or margarine, at room temperature
- 2 ounces jack cheese, thinly sliced
- 2 fresh or drained canned pineapple slices
- 1 teaspoon brown sugar
  Ground nutmeg
- 4 ounces thinly sliced cooked ham

Spread one side of each bread slice with butter. Place half the cheese on unbuttered sides of 2 bread slices, then top each with a pineapple slice. Sprinkle evenly with sugar and nutmeg; top with ham, dividing equally. Cover with remaining bread slices, buttered sides up.

Place sandwiches in a wide nonstick frying pan over medium heat. Cover and cook, turning once, until cheese is melted and bread is toasted (about 5 minutes). Cut sandwiches in half diagonally and serve immediately. Makes 2 servings.

Per serving: 429 calories, 25 g protein, 39 g carbohydrates, 20 g total fat, 74 mg cholesterol, 1,342 mg sodium

Light & Hearty Soups

Pictured on facing page

Cool Avocado Gazpacho

Preparation time: About 20 minutes

Chilling time: At least 2 hours

Cooking time (for croutons): About 11 minutes

The beguiling interplay of crisp, spicy croutons and smooth, cool avocados distinguishes this soup. To achieve a silken texture, use a blender (rather than a food processor) to purée the avocado chunks and chopped cucumber. Follow the soup with Spanish rice and sautéed chicken breasts topped with salsa.

- 1 **small cucumber, peeled and coarsely chopped**
- 1¾ **cups chicken broth**
- 2 **tablespoons chopped cilantro**
- 1 **tablespoon lime juice**
- 1 **medium-size firm-ripe avocado, pitted, peeled, and coarsely chopped**
  Chili-Garlic Croutons (recipe follows)
- 2 **tablespoons chopped red onion**
  Cilantro sprigs (optional)
- 1 **medium-size lime, cut into wedges**

In a blender or food processor, combine cucumber, broth, chopped cilantro, and lime juice; whirl until smoothly puréed. Add half the chopped avocado and whirl until smooth; then add remaining avocado and whirl briefly just until coarsely puréed (leave some chunks). Cover and refrigerate until cool (at least 2 hours) or until next day.

Meanwhile, prepare Chili-Garlic Croutons.

To serve, pour soup into 2 wide, shallow bowls. Garnish each serving with croutons, onion, and, if desired, cilantro sprigs. Offer lime wedges to squeeze into soup. Makes 2 servings.

Chili-Garlic Croutons. Cut enough ½-inch cubes from a loaf of **French bread** to make 1 cup. Spread bread cubes in a pie pan and bake in a 400° oven until golden and crisp (about 10 minutes); remove from oven.

Melt 2 tablespoons **butter** or margarine in a medium-size frying pan over medium heat. Stir in 1 clove **garlic** (minced or pressed) and ¾ teaspoon **chili powder**; cook, stirring, for 1 minute. Add croutons and stir until evenly coated with butter mixture. Remove from heat and let cool. If made ahead, store airtight at room temperature for up to 1 day.

Per serving: 369 calories, 7 g protein, 26 g carbohydrates, 29 g total fat, 32 mg cholesterol, 1,109 mg sodium

*A warm summer evening invites patio dining—and Cool
Avocado Gazpacho (recipe on facing page) is the ideal beginning for an
al fresco meal. Chili-seasoned croutons and chopped onion add a piquant
accent to the smooth soup; a squeeze of fresh lime is the final
touch. Sip chilled white wine alongside.*

15

Iced Carrot & Orange Soup

Preparation time: About 15 minutes

Cooking time: About 35 minutes

Chilling time: At least 4 hours

Served ice cold, this velvety golden blend of carrots and fresh orange juice is the perfect opener for a spicy meal. You might sip it from small mugs while Tandoori Barbecued Chicken (page 48) cooks on the grill.

1	tablespoon butter or margarine
8	ounces carrots, thinly sliced
1	medium-size onion, thinly sliced
1½	cups chicken broth
½	teaspoon sugar
¼	teaspoon dry dill weed
¾	cup fresh orange juice
	Salt
	Dill sprigs and grated orange peel

Melt butter in a 2- to 3-quart pan over medium heat. Add carrots and onion; cook, stirring often, until onion is golden (about 10 minutes). Add broth, sugar, and dill weed. Bring to a boil over high heat; reduce heat, cover, and simmer until carrots are very tender to bite (about 25 minutes).

Whirl carrot mixture, a portion at a time, in a blender or food processor until smooth; add orange juice and whirl again. Season to taste with salt. Cover and refrigerate for at least 4 hours or until next day.

To serve, stir well; pour into 2 bowls. Garnish with dill sprigs and orange peel. Makes 2 servings.

Per serving: 180 calories, 5 g protein, 26 g carbohydrates, 7 g total fat, 16 mg cholesterol, 840 mg sodium

Acorn Curry Soup

Preparation time: About 15 minutes

Cooking time: About 50 minutes

Most of the cooking in this recipe is done, unattended, in the oven. Start by baking a small acorn squash with onion, curry powder, and a little red pepper; then purée it with broth to make a thick, creamy soup. Serve with Wilted Spinach Salad with Oranges (page 25) and warm pita breads for a satisfying lunch or supper.

1	small acorn squash (about 1½ lbs.)
1	tablespoon butter or margarine
¾	teaspoon curry powder
⅛	teaspoon crushed red pepper flakes
1	medium-size onion, thinly sliced
1½	cups chicken broth
2	tablespoons sour cream or plain lowfat yogurt
	Watercress sprigs (optional)

Cut squash in half lengthwise; scoop out and discard seeds.

Place butter in a 7- by 11-inch baking dish and set dish in a 350° oven until butter is melted. Add curry powder, pepper flakes, and onion; stir until onion is well coated. Lay squash halves, cut sides down, in dish. Bake until squash is tender when pierced (about 45 minutes).

Let squash stand until cool enough to touch. Scoop flesh from peel; discard peel. In a blender or food processor, whirl squash, onion mixture from baking dish, and broth until smoothly puréed. Pour purée into a 2- to 3-quart pan and stir over medium-high heat until hot (about 5 minutes).

To serve, ladle soup into 2 bowls. Stir sour cream until smooth; then carefully spoon a 2-inch strip of sour cream over center of each serving. Swirl sour cream with tip of a sharp knife to make a pretty pattern. Garnish soup with watercress, if desired. Makes 2 servings.

Per serving: 222 calories, 5 g protein, 32 g carbohydrates, 10 g total fat, 22 mg cholesterol, 815 mg sodium

pple Cheese Soup

Preparation time: About 15 minutes

Cooking time: About 13 minutes

Apples and cheese are natural companions; here, they come together in a slightly sweet soup that's hard to resist. Enhance the flavor with tangy chutney, either spooned into each bowlful or spread on crackers to serve alongside. Follow the soup with a hearty main course, such as Cabbage-Paprika Stroganoff (page 40), and green beans.

- 1½ **cups chicken broth**
- 2 **cups peeled, chopped apples, such as McIntosh, Red Delicious, or Golden Delicious (about 2 medium-size apples)**
- 2 **tablespoons slivered almonds**
- 1 **tablespoon butter or margarine**
- 1 **tablespoon all-purpose flour**
- ½ **cup apple juice**
- ½ **cup packed shredded Cheddar cheese**
- 2 **tablespoons chutney**

In a 2- to 3-quart pan, combine broth and apples. Bring to a boil over high heat; then reduce heat, cover, and simmer until apples are tender when pierced (about 10 minutes).

Meanwhile, toast almonds in a small frying pan over medium heat until golden (about 3 minutes), stirring often. Remove from heat and set aside.

Pour apples and broth into a blender or food processor; whirl until smoothly puréed, then set aside. Melt butter in apple cooking pan over medium-high heat. Add flour and stir until bubbly (about 1 minute), then remove from heat and slowly whisk in apple juice. Cook, stirring, until thickened (about 2 minutes). Remove pan from heat. Stir in half the cheese, then all the apple purée; stir mixture over medium-high heat just until boiling.

To serve, ladle soup into 2 bowls; sprinkle each serving with half each of the almonds and remaining cheese. Offer chutney to stir into soup to taste. Makes 2 servings.

Per serving: 383 calories, 12 g protein, 40 g carbohydrates, 21 g total fat, 45 mg cholesterol, 1,011 mg sodium

roccoli-Buttermilk Soup

Copied

Preparation time: About 15 minutes

Cooking time: About 17 minutes

Buttermilk adds a pleasant tartness and a creamy texture (but very little fat) to this nourishing first-course soup. Try it as the lead-in to a homespun meal of meat loaf, mashed potatoes, and crisp tossed salad.

- 8 **ounces broccoli**
- 1½ **cups beef broth**
- 1 **small onion, quartered**
- ½ **teaspoon dry basil**
- ¼ **teaspoon sugar**
- 1 **clove garlic, minced or pressed**
- 1 **cup buttermilk**
  Salt and pepper
  Paprika

Cut flowerets off broccoli. Cut off and discard tough ends of stalks; thinly slice tender sections of stalks. In a 2- to 3-quart pan, combine broccoli stalks and flowerets, broth, onion, basil, sugar, and garlic. Bring to a boil over high heat; then reduce heat, cover, and simmer until broccoli is tender to bite (about 15 minutes).

Whirl broccoli mixture, a portion at a time, in a blender or food processor until smooth. Return to pan and whisk in buttermilk; heat until steaming (about 2 minutes). Season to taste with salt and pepper.

To serve, ladle soup into 2 bowls; sprinkle each serving with paprika. Makes 2 servings.

Per serving: 97 calories, 8 g protein, 13 g carbohydrates, 2 g total fat, 5 mg cholesterol, 768 mg sodium

When it's chilly outside, stay cozy indoors with a good book,
good company, and steaming bowls of Eggs & Bacon Vegetable Soup (recipe
on facing page). Toasted slices of hearty bread, ripe winter pears, and mugs
of hot tea round out a lunch that will keep you warm all day long.

18

Eggs & Bacon Vegetable Soup

Preparation time: About 15 minutes

Cooking time: About 25 minutes

Quick but nourishing, this soup is an ideal lunch for a rainy day. The eggs do double duty, adding protein to the dish as well as enriching the broth. Serve with whole-grain toast and ripe pears or other fresh fruit.

- 4 slices bacon (about 4 oz. *total*), finely diced
- 1 medium-size carrot, thinly sliced
- 1 small onion, chopped
- 1 small turnip, peeled and diced
- 1 small thin-skinned potato, peeled and diced
- 1 teaspoon dry basil
- 1¾ cups chicken broth
- 1 cup lightly packed torn spinach leaves, rinsed and drained
- 1 small can (about 8 oz.) stewed tomatoes
   Salt and pepper
- 2 eggs

Cook bacon in a small frying pan over medium heat until crisp (about 5 minutes), stirring often. Lift out with a slotted spoon, drain, and set aside.

In a 2- to 3-quart pan, combine carrot, onion, turnip, potato, basil, and broth. Cover and bring to a boil; then reduce heat and simmer until all vegetables are tender when pierced (about 10 minutes). Meanwhile, finely chop spinach.

Uncover soup, stir in spinach and tomatoes, and cook until spinach is wilted (about 2 minutes); season to taste with salt and pepper.

Crack eggs, one at a time, into a saucer; gently slide eggs into soup. Cover pan and simmer, without stirring, until eggs are cooked to your liking (about 8 minutes for firm yolks).

To serve, ladle soup into 2 wide, shallow bowls, placing one egg in each bowl. Sprinkle soup with bacon. Makes 2 servings.

Per serving: 307 calories, 18 g protein, 28 g carbohydrates, 14 g total fat, 226 mg cholesterol, 1,540 mg sodium

Fresh Ravioli & Cabbage Soup

Preparation time: About 15 minutes

Cooking time: About 13 minutes

Clear beef broth, a few vegetables, and fresh ravioli from your market's deli case add up to a delightful main-dish soup. To round out the menu, offer hot homemade biscuits and a wedge of Asiago cheese. (For the soup, you need only half a standard-size package of ravioli; serve the remainder as an easy pasta course the following night.)

- 3 slices bacon (about 3 oz. *total*), diced
- 1 small onion, finely chopped
- 1 clove garlic, minced or pressed
- 1 tablespoon chopped parsley
- 2 cups beef broth
- 1 cup water
- 1 medium-size carrot, thinly sliced
   Half of 1 package (about 9 oz.) fresh meat-filled ravioli
- 1 cup finely shredded cabbage
   Freshly ground pepper
   Grated Parmesan cheese

Cook bacon in a 3- to 4-quart pan over medium heat until translucent and limp (about 3 minutes), stirring often. Add onion; continue to cook, stirring, until onion and bacon are lightly browned (about 5 more minutes). Spoon off and discard bacon drippings from pan, then stir in garlic and parsley. Add broth, water, and carrot. Increase heat to high and bring soup to a boil.

Add ravioli and cabbage to pan. Reduce heat to medium and boil gently, stirring occasionally, until ravioli are just tender to bite (about 5 minutes). Season to taste with pepper.

To serve, ladle soup into 2 bowls; offer cheese to add to taste. Makes 2 servings.

Per serving: 314 calories, 16 g protein, 28 g carbohydrates, 16 g total fat, 60 mg cholesterol, 1,306 mg sodium

Butter Bean & Ham Chowder

Preparation time: About 15 minutes

Cooking time: About 14 minutes

This light chowder is filling, too, thanks to a generous helping of large, tender butter beans. Served with toasted jack cheese sandwiches and a dessert of baked apples, it's just right for supper on a blustery day.

1	tablespoon butter or margarine
½	cup thinly sliced green onions
1	medium-size carrot, chopped
1	tablespoon all-purpose flour
1½	cups chicken broth
½	cup milk
½	teaspoon dry marjoram
2	ounces thinly sliced cooked ham
1	can (about 15 oz.) butter beans, drained
1	cup fresh or frozen corn kernels
	Pepper

Melt butter in a 2- to 3-quart pan over medium-high heat. Add onions and carrot and cook, stirring occasionally, until onions are limp (about 3 minutes). Add flour; stir until bubbly (about 1 minute).

Add broth, milk, and marjoram; stir well. Bring to a boil; then reduce heat, cover, and simmer until carrot is tender to bite (about 5 minutes). Meanwhile, cut ham into long, thin strips.

When carrot is tender, add ham, beans, and corn. Cover and continue to simmer until soup is heated (about 5 more minutes). Season to taste with pepper; ladle into 2 bowls. Makes 2 servings.

Per serving: 411 calories, 25 g protein, 54 g carbohydrates, 13 g total fat, 41 mg cholesterol, 1,944 mg sodium

Lean Fish & Pasta Chowder

Preparation time: About 15 minutes

Cooking time: About 22 minutes

Frozen fish poached in homemade tomato-vegetable soup provides a convenient solution to the problem of preparing a quick meal that's healthful, too. You can use any lean white-fleshed fish; select the type that suits your taste and budget best. Pair the chowder with a green salad and crusty bread.

1	tablespoon olive oil
1	small onion, thinly sliced
1	small carrot, thinly sliced
2	tablespoons minced parsley
½	teaspoon dry tarragon
¼	teaspoon pepper
6	ounces frozen boneless, skinless white-fleshed fish fillets (such as sole, ocean perch, cod, haddock, or orange roughy), slightly thawed
1	bottle (about 8 oz.) clam juice
¾	cup tomato juice
¼	cup water
⅓	cup small shell-shaped pasta

Heat oil in a 2- to 3-quart pan over medium heat. Add onion, carrot, parsley, tarragon, and pepper; cook, stirring often, until onion is limp (about 7 minutes). Meanwhile, rinse fish, pat dry, and cut into 1-inch chunks. Set aside.

Stir clam juice, tomato juice, and water into vegetable mixture. Increase heat to high and bring mixture to a boil; add pasta, reduce heat, cover, and simmer for 10 minutes. Add fish, cover, and continue to simmer until fish is just opaque but still moist in center; cut to test (about 5 more minutes). Ladle soup into 2 bowls and serve immediately. Makes 2 servings.

Per serving: 234 calories, 20 g protein, 20 g carbohydrates, 8 g total fat, 41 mg cholesterol, 670 mg sodium

Tomato-Seafood Bisque

Preparation time: About 15 minutes

Cooking time: About 7 minutes

Treat your dinner partner to an exquisite seafood soup, tailored to his or her liking. Begin by making a rich, clam-filled tomato broth; then add scallops, shrimp, or chunks of mild white fish (or a combination of all three). To complete the feast, offer warm sourdough bread and a shellfish appetizer, such as shrimp cocktail or oysters on the half shell.

1   can (about 6 oz.) minced clams
1   cup chicken broth
¾   cup tomato juice
¼   cup dry white wine
1   tablespoon dry sherry
¼   teaspoon dry oregano
2   medium-size firm-ripe tomatoes, peeled, seeded, and chopped
2   cloves garlic, minced or pressed

8   ounces scallops, shelled and deveined raw shrimp, or boneless, skinless white-fleshed fish fillets (such as halibut, lingcod, or orange roughy), cut into bite-size pieces
¼   cup whipping cream
¼   cup finely chopped parsley
    Liquid hot pepper seasoning
    Salt

In a 2- to 3-quart pan, combine clams and their liquid, broth, tomato juice, wine, sherry, oregano, tomatoes, and garlic. Bring to a boil over high heat; reduce heat, cover, and simmer until tomatoes are soft (about 5 minutes). Stir in scallops and cream. Bring to a gentle boil and cook just until scallops are opaque in center; cut to test (about 2 minutes).

Remove from heat; stir in parsley. Season to taste with hot pepper seasoning and salt, then ladle into 2 bowls. Makes 2 servings.

Per serving: 345 calories, 35 g protein, 18 g carbohydrates, 12 g total fat, 100 mg cholesterol, 1,081 mg sodium

Chinese Chicken & Shrimp Soup

Preparation time: About 15 minutes

Cooking time: About 5 minutes

Filled with tiny shrimp, cubes of chicken breast, and barely cooked vegetables, this Asian-inspired soup makes an incredibly light, fresh-tasting main course. Serve purchased pot stickers with the soup, then conclude the meal with pineapple sorbet and crisp gingersnaps.

3   cups chicken broth
1   tablespoon minced fresh ginger
1½ teaspoons soy sauce
1   boneless, skinless chicken breast half (about 4 oz.), cut into ½-inch cubes
2   ounces mushrooms, sliced
1   small head baby bok choy, trimmed and thinly sliced (about 1 cup)
½   cup diced firm tofu

¼   cup sliced green onions
4   ounces small cooked shrimp
2   tablespoons chopped cilantro
    Ground red pepper (cayenne) or chili oil (optional)

In a 2- to 3-quart pan, combine broth, ginger, and soy sauce; bring to a boil over high heat. Add chicken, mushrooms, bok choy, tofu, and onions. Return to a boil. Then reduce heat, cover, and simmer until mushrooms are soft and chicken is no longer pink in center; cut to test (about 5 minutes).

Remove from heat and stir in shrimp and cilantro. Season to taste with red pepper, if desired; then ladle into 2 bowls. Makes 2 servings.

Per serving: 270 calories, 41 g protein, 8 g carbohydrates, 9 g total fat, 144 mg cholesterol, 1,935 mg sodium

Hot & Cold Salads

Pictured on facing page

Warm Goat Cheese & Apple Salad

Preparation time: About 20 minutes

Cooking time: About 20 minutes

Simple but by no means plain, this hot-and-cold salad was inspired by a first course popular in France. Sweet apple slices, butter lettuce, and small broiled goat cheeses are topped with honey-mustard vinaigrette and accompanied by crunchy homemade breadsticks. (You'll find ripened goat cheese in specialty food stores and cheese shops.) For a bistro-style menu, follow the salad with Coq au Vin with Rice (page 49).

　　Honey-Mustard Dressing (recipe follows)
　　Baguette Batons (recipe follows)
1　medium-size red apple
1　tablespoon lemon juice
4　large butter lettuce leaves, rinsed and crisped
2　round, firm ripened goat cheeses, such as crottin or chavignon (about 2 oz. *each*)
　　Coarsely ground pepper

Prepare Honey-Mustard Dressing and set aside.

　　Prepare Baguette Batons. While batons are baking, quarter and core apple; then cut each quarter lengthwise into ⅓-inch-thick slices. In a small bowl, gently mix apple with lemon juice. Arrange lettuce leaves on 2 salad plates; top lettuce with apple slices. Set aside.

　　Place cheeses in a pie pan and broil 2 inches below heat until softened and lightly browned (about 5 minutes). With a spatula, transfer one cheese to each salad. Spoon dressing over salads; season to taste with pepper. Serve with Baguette Batons. Makes 2 servings.

Honey-Mustard Dressing. In a small bowl, whisk together 2 tablespoons *each* **salad oil** and **cider vinegar,** 2 teaspoons **honey,** and 1 tablespoon **Dijon mustard.**

Baguette Batons. Cut 1 small **baguette** (about 4 oz.) in half crosswise. Cut one half lengthwise into quarters (reserve remaining half of loaf for other uses). Place quarters, cut sides up, on a baking sheet; brush cut sides with 2 tablespoons **butter** or margarine, melted. Bake in a 350° oven until golden (about 15 minutes).

Per serving: 588 calories, 14 g protein, 39 g carbohydrates, 43 g total fat, 84 mg cholesterol, 859 mg sodium

Dining French style means starting with the salad. Here, it's
Warm Goat Cheese & Apple Salad (recipe on facing page): vinaigrette-
dressed fruit, cheese, and greens with buttery baguette breadsticks.
Add chunky tumblers of robust red wine for a first course
that's truly magnifique.

23

Wilted Romaine with Spicy Sausage Dressing

Preparation time: About 20 minutes

Cooking time: About 6 minutes

Turn a bowlful of typical salad makings into an intriguing new dish with the addition of a few exotic ingredients. Aromatic fish sauce, fresh lime juice, and sautéed *lop cheong*—a flavorful Chinese sausage—combine to make an unusual dressing for crisp greens. To carry out the Oriental theme, complete the meal with Chinese Chicken & Shrimp Soup (page 21).

    Lime Dressing (recipe follows)
2 **cups bite-size pieces romaine lettuce, rinsed and crisped**
½ **small cucumber, peeled and thinly sliced**
1 **medium-size tomato, cut into wedges**
4 **thin slices red onion, separated into rings**
½ **cup lightly packed cilantro sprigs**

⅓ **pound (4 or 5) Chinese sausages (lop cheong), cut into ¼-inch-thick slanting slices; or ⅓ pound thinly sliced dry salami, cut into strips**
2 **tablespoons salad oil**
3 **cloves garlic, minced or pressed**

Prepare Lime Dressing and set aside. In a large bowl, combine lettuce, cucumber, tomato, onion, and cilantro. Set aside.

Place sausages and oil in a wide frying pan or wok over medium heat; cook, stirring often, until meat is lightly browned (about 4 minutes). Add garlic; stir just until golden (about 30 seconds). Add Lime Dressing; stir just to heat through (about 1 minute). Pour sausage mixture over lettuce mixture; toss lightly. Makes 2 servings.

Lime Dressing. Mix ⅓ cup **fresh lime juice,** 1 tablespoon **fish sauce** (*nam pla*) or soy sauce, and ½ teaspoon **crushed red pepper flakes.**

Per serving: 506 calories, 21 g protein, 16 g carbohydrates, 41 g total fat, 59 mg cholesterol, 1,408 mg sodium

Hot Beef & Watercress Salad

Preparation time: About 15 minutes

Marinating time: At least 30 minutes

Cooking time: About 3 minutes

Garlicky stir-fried beef atop a bed of peppery watercress is a welcome dinner choice at any time of year. The dish gets its lasting appeal from a tempting interplay of textures and temperatures—crisp with chewy, hot with cool. You might serve bowls of brown rice alongside, then finish the meal with a fruit dessert such as fresh pineapple.

8 **ounces lean boneless top round, flank steak, or sirloin steak (about 1 inch thick)**
4 **cloves garlic, minced or pressed**
2 **teaspoons soy sauce**
1 **teaspoon sugar**
1 **tablespoon salad oil**
2 **tablespoons white wine vinegar**
¼ **teaspoon pepper**

1 **small white onion, thinly sliced and separated into rings**
3 **cups lightly packed watercress sprigs, rinsed and crisped**

Cut beef with the grain into 3-inch-wide strips; then cut each strip across the grain into ⅛-inch-thick slanting slices. In a bowl, stir together garlic, soy sauce, ½ teaspoon of the sugar, and 1 teaspoon of the oil. Add beef and stir to coat well.

In another bowl, stir together remaining ½ teaspoon sugar, remaining 2 teaspoons oil, vinegar, and pepper. Add onion and mix lightly.

Cover beef and onion mixtures; refrigerate for at least 30 minutes or until next day. Shortly before serving, add watercress to onion mixture; mix lightly to coat. Divide between 2 dinner plates.

Place a wide frying pan or wok over high heat. When pan is hot, add beef mixture; cook, stirring, until meat is browned (about 3 minutes). Spoon meat mixture atop salads. Makes 2 servings.

Per serving: 241 calories, 28 g protein, 8 g carbohydrates, 11 g total fat, 65 mg cholesterol, 428 mg sodium

Italian-style Grilled Fish Salad

Preparation time: About 20 minutes

Grilling time: About 5 minutes

Skewers of grilled swordfish top arugula, olives, and orange slices in this bold-flavored entrée. Try it on a warm evening, perhaps with chilled white wine and Iced Carrot & Orange Soup (page 16).

- 1 large orange
- 3 cups lightly packed arugula or watercress sprigs, rinsed and crisped
- 8 plain melba toast rounds
- 2 thin slices red onion, separated into rings
- ¼ cup drained oil-cured black olives (such as Kalamata) or small ripe olives
- 3 tablespoons red wine vinegar
- ¼ cup olive oil
- 1 teaspoon chopped fresh thyme or ½ teaspoon dry thyme
- 1 teaspoon anchovy paste (optional)
- 8 to 12 ounces boned, skinned swordfish or wahoo (also called ono), cut into 1-inch chunks

Grate 1 teaspoon peel (colored part only) from orange; set aside. With a sharp knife, cut remaining peel and all white membrane from outside of orange; thinly slice orange crosswise. Divide arugula between 2 dinner plates, then alternate melba toast, onion rings, and orange slices over greens. Scatter olives over salads.

In a small bowl, stir together grated orange peel, vinegar, oil, thyme, and anchovy paste (if used). Spoon out and reserve 2 tablespoons of the dressing for basting fish; set remaining dressing aside.

Thread fish on two 10-inch-long metal skewers; brush lightly with some of the reserved 2 tablespoons dressing. Place fish on a lightly greased grill 4 to 6 inches above a solid bed of hot coals. Cook, brushing once or twice with reserved dressing and turning once, until fish is just opaque but still moist in center; cut to test (about 5 minutes).

To serve, place skewers atop salads; spoon remaining dressing over salads. Makes 2 servings.

Per serving: 559 calories, 32 g protein, 21 g carbohydrates, 40 g total fat, 55 mg cholesterol, 743 mg sodium

Wilted Spinach Salad with Oranges

Preparation time: About 15 minutes

Cooking time: About 11 minutes

The traditional wilted spinach salad just doesn't fit into today's leaner menus. For a lighter version, replace the standard heavy bacon dressing with a blend of vinegar-infused onions, fresh oranges, and a touch of oil. Pair the salad with Grilled Turkey on Sesame Buns (page 51) for a super-nutritious supper.

- 2 medium-size oranges
- 1 small onion, thinly sliced
- ¼ cup balsamic or red wine vinegar
- 1 tablespoon salad oil
- ½ teaspoon dry tarragon
- 4 cups lightly packed torn spinach leaves, rinsed and crisped
  Coarsely ground pepper

Grate 1 teaspoon peel (colored part only) from one of the oranges; place grated peel in a medium-size frying pan and set oranges aside. To pan, add onion, vinegar, oil, and tarragon. Place over low heat, cover, and cook until onion is tender to bite (about 10 minutes).

Meanwhile, with a sharp knife, cut peel and all white membrane from outside of oranges. Holding fruit over a bowl to catch juice, cut between membranes to free segments.

When onion is cooked, add orange segments and any juice to pan; cook, stirring, just until oranges are hot (about 1 minute). Place spinach in a salad bowl and pour orange mixture over it; toss to mix well. Season to taste with pepper. Makes 2 servings.

Per serving: 169 calories, 5 g protein, 24 g carbohydrates, 8 g total fat, 0 mg cholesterol, 95 mg sodium

Celebrate a sunny day with a stunning lunch on the deck:
Cracked Crab & Yellow Rice Salad (recipe on facing page), frosty drinks,
and a bowl of glistening strawberries. Tender asparagus and a simple rice
mixture, both seasoned with tangy mustard-turmeric dressing, accompany
a whole Dungeness crab for an unforgettable entrée.

Asparagus & Prosciutto Salad

Preparation time: About 10 minutes

Cooking time: About 9 minutes

Fit for a celebration, this sophisticated first course features slender asparagus spears drizzled with a warm dressing of slivered prosciutto, lemon, and garlic. Choose an Italian-style second course, too; you might try veal scaloppine with herb-sprinkled pasta bow ties.

8	ounces asparagus, tough ends removed
3	thin slices prosciutto (about 2 oz. *total*), slivered
2½	tablespoons olive oil
1	clove garlic, minced or pressed
3	tablespoons lemon juice
1	teaspoon Dijon mustard
1	lemon, cut into 4 wedges

Peel asparagus stalks, if desired. In a wide frying pan, bring 1 inch of water to a boil over high heat. Add asparagus and cook just until tender-crisp to bite (about 4 minutes). Drain, immerse in ice water until cool, and drain again. Divide asparagus between 2 salad plates.

In a small frying pan, combine prosciutto, 1½ teaspoons of the oil, and garlic. Cook over medium-high heat, stirring, until prosciutto curls and garlic is golden (about 5 minutes). Remove from heat and stir in lemon juice, mustard, and remaining 2 tablespoons oil. Spoon dressing over asparagus; offer lemon wedges to squeeze over asparagus to taste. Makes 2 servings.

Per serving: 234 calories, 9 g protein, 10 g carbohydrates, 20 g total fat, 17 mg cholesterol, 703 mg sodium

Pictured on facing page

Cracked Crab & Yellow Rice Salad

Preparation time: About 30 minutes

Cooking time: About 4 minutes

On a warm afternoon, set out a handsome feast of cracked crab, tender-crisp asparagus, and ocher-hued rice. Ground turmeric gives the rice its vivid color and subtle flavor. Sesame-sprinkled dinner rolls, white wine spritzers, and a bowl of fresh ripe strawberries complete a wonderful spring or summer luncheon.

	Turmeric Dressing (recipe follows)
1	large cooked Dungeness crab (about 2½ lbs.), cleaned and cracked (save uncracked back shell); or 8 to 12 ounces cooked crabmeat
8	ounces asparagus, tough ends removed
1½	cups cold cooked long-grain white rice
⅓	cup thinly sliced green onions
	Salt and pepper
	Parsley sprigs and lemon slices

Prepare Turmeric Dressing and set aside.

Rinse crab back shell; set aside. Remove meat from body of crab; discard shells. Mound crabmeat on one side of a large platter; arrange unshelled legs and claws around meat. Top with reserved back shell; refrigerate.

Peel asparagus stalks, if desired. In a wide frying pan, bring 1 inch of water to a boil over high heat. Add asparagus and cook just until tender-crisp to bite (about 4 minutes). Drain, immerse in ice water until cool, and drain again. Arrange asparagus on platter with crab. Spoon about a third of the Turmeric Dressing over asparagus.

Mix remaining Turmeric Dressing with rice and onions; season to taste with salt and pepper. Mound rice mixture on platter. Garnish with parsley sprigs and lemon slices. Makes 2 servings.

Turmeric Dressing. In a small bowl, whisk together ⅓ cup **salad oil**, 2 tablespoons **white wine vinegar**, 2 teaspoons **Dijon mustard**, and ½ teaspoon **ground turmeric**.

Per serving: 631 calories, 34 g protein, 35 g carbohydrates, 39 g total fat, 142 mg cholesterol, 550 mg sodium

Lobster Salad with Ginger Dressing

Preparation time: About 25 minutes

Cooking time: About 12 minutes

Usually sold frozen, lobster tails are easier to handle than the whole shellfish; and when combined with other ingredients—as in this light main course—just one tail makes two ample servings. (If you like, substitute whole shrimp for lobster to vary the presentation.) Cold lemonade and breadsticks with butter nicely complement the salad.

     Ginger Dressing (recipe follows)

4 **ounces Chinese pea pods (also called snow peas), ends and strings removed**

1 **lobster tail (6 to 8 oz.), thawed if frozen; or 8 ounces medium-size raw shrimp, shelled and deveined**

4 **cups bite-size pieces butter lettuce, rinsed and crisped**

1 **large firm-ripe kiwi fruit, peeled and thinly sliced**

2 **preserved kumquats, thinly sliced**

Prepare Ginger Dressing and set aside.

In a 4- to 6-quart pan, bring about 2 quarts water to a boil over high heat. Add pea pods and cook just until tender-crisp to bite (about 2 minutes). Lift out with a slotted spoon and immerse in ice water until cool; then drain and set aside.

Return water in pan to a boil. Add lobster tail or shrimp, reduce heat, and simmer, uncovered, until meat is opaque in thickest part; cut to test (about 10 minutes for lobster, about 4 minutes for shrimp). Drain shellfish, immerse in ice water until cool, and drain again.

With kitchen scissors, clip fins from sides of soft undershell of lobster tail; then snip along edges. Lift off and discard undershell. Working from body end, carefully remove meat from shell in one piece. Thinly slice meat crosswise.

Divide lettuce, kiwi fruit, kumquats, lobster, and pea pods between 2 dinner plates. Top salads with Ginger Dressing. Makes 2 servings.

Ginger Dressing. In a small bowl, whisk together ½ teaspoon finely shredded **orange peel**, ½ cup **orange juice**, 1 tablespoon **sherry or red wine vinegar,** and 1 tablespoon minced **crystallized ginger.**

Per serving: 204 calories, 15 g protein, 35 g carbohydrates, 1 g total fat, 39 mg cholesterol, 245 mg sodium

Avocado, Zucchini & Arugula Salad

Preparation time: About 15 minutes

Arugula adds peppery tang to this all-green, super-simple vegetable salad. Partnered with crusty Italian bread and a wedge of fontina cheese, it makes a light but satisfying lunch.

1 **medium-size zucchini, coarsely shredded**

1 **small avocado, pitted, peeled, and sliced**

1 **cup lightly packed arugula or watercress sprigs, rinsed and crisped**

¼ **cup extra-virgin olive oil**

3 **tablespoons lemon juice**
    Salt and pepper

6 **Greek or other oil-cured black olives (such as Kalamata), optional**

Place zucchini in a wide, shallow bowl. Arrange avocado and arugula over zucchini.

Stir together oil and lemon juice, pour over salad, and mix well. Season to taste with salt and pepper. Spoon onto 2 plates; garnish each serving with olives, if desired. Makes 2 servings.

Per serving: 380 calories, 3 g protein, 10 g carbohydrates, 40 g total fat, 0 mg cholesterol, 24 mg sodium

Fennel Salad with Oranges

Preparation time: About 15 minutes

Cooking time: About 4 minutes

Chilling time: 15 minutes

Raw fennel has a faint licorice flavor and a crisp, celerylike texture; when tossed with oranges, toasted pine nuts, and lettuce, it's a superb accompaniment for veal chops or a hearty risotto. You'll find fresh fennel in produce stores and some supermarkets from late fall until spring.

- 2 tablespoons pine nuts or slivered almonds
- 2 medium-size oranges
- 2 tablespoons salad oil
- 1 tablespoon white wine vinegar
- ½ teaspoon minced fresh rosemary or ½ teaspoon dry rosemary, crumbled
- 1 large head fresh fennel (about 1 lb.)
- 2 large butter lettuce leaves, rinsed and crisped
  Salt and pepper

Toast pine nuts in a small frying pan over medium heat until golden (about 4 minutes), stirring often. Let cool.

Grate ¼ teaspoon peel (colored part only) from one of the oranges; set aside. Squeeze enough juice from same orange to make ¼ cup. With a sharp knife, cut peel and all white membrane from outside of remaining orange; thinly slice orange crosswise and set aside.

In a bowl, stir together grated orange peel, orange juice, oil, vinegar, and rosemary. Set aside.

Remove and reserve fennel leaves; cut off tough stems. Trim bruises from fennel, then cut head into quarters lengthwise; remove and discard core. Thinly slice quarters crosswise; mix with dressing in bowl. Cover; refrigerate for 15 minutes.

Place lettuce on 2 salad plates. Top with fennel mixture, oranges, pine nuts, and fennel leaves. Season with salt and pepper. Makes 2 servings.

Per serving: 253 calories, 6 g protein, 20 g carbohydrates, 19 g total fat, 0 mg cholesterol, 206 mg sodium

Sesame Chicken Salad

Preparation time: About 20 minutes

Cooking time: About 12 minutes

Light in calories but full of flavor, this entrée salad of tender steeped chicken and crisp vegetables is a winning choice for a poolside lunch or any other warm-weather meal. Offer tall glasses of spicy tomato juice and a basket of toasted pita triangles alongside.

- 2 boneless, skinless chicken breast halves (about 8 oz. *total*)
- 1 tablespoon sesame seeds
  Soy Dressing (recipe follows)
- 2 large celery stalks, cut into thin slanting slices
- 1 medium-size red bell pepper, seeded and cut into thin strips
- 1 can (about 8 oz.) sliced water chestnuts, drained
- 2 green onions, cut into long, thin slivers
- 2 small celery stalks with leaves

Rinse and drain chicken; set aside. In a 2- to 3-quart pan, bring about 4 cups water to a boil over high heat. Add chicken, cover pan tightly, and remove from heat. Let stand until meat in thickest part is no longer pink; cut to test (about 12 minutes). Lift out chicken and let cool, then tear meat into shreds.

While chicken is steeping, toast sesame seeds in a small frying pan over medium heat until golden (about 4 minutes), shaking pan often. Let cool. Prepare Soy Dressing and set aside.

In a bowl, mix chicken, sliced celery, bell pepper, and water chestnuts; pour in Soy Dressing and mix well. Divide salad between 2 dinner plates; sprinkle with onions and sesame seeds. Garnish each salad with a celery stalk. Makes 2 servings.

Soy Dressing. Mix 3 tablespoons **rice vinegar** (or 3 tablespoons white wine vinegar plus 2 teaspoons sugar); 2 tablespoons **soy sauce**; 1 tablespoon **Oriental sesame oil**; 1½ tablespoons minced **fresh ginger**; and 1 clove **garlic**, minced or pressed.

Per serving: 331 calories, 30 g protein, 29 g carbohydrates, 11 g total fat, 66 mg cholesterol, 1,186 mg sodium

Pasta Every Way

Pictured on facing page

Asian-style Pasta Primavera

Preparation time: About 15 minutes

Cooking time: About 9 minutes

In a recipe title, the word "primavera" describes a dish made with an abundance of spring vegetables. This Asian-style interpretation of *pasta primavera* features stir-fried baby bok choy, shiitake mushrooms, and crisp pea pods over slender noodles. Complete a light supper with chilled white wine and tender greens in Herb Vinaigrette (page 44).

   3   **large fresh shiitake mushrooms, *each* about 3 inches in diameter; or 2 ounces large fresh regular mushrooms**

   ¾   **cup chicken broth**

   1   **tablespoon soy sauce**

   ½   **teaspoon *each* sugar and wine vinegar**

   2   **tablespoons sesame seeds**

   8   **ounces dry capellini (angel hair pasta)**

   2   **tablespoons salad oil**

   2   **ounces thinly sliced cooked ham, cut into julienne strips**

   2   **cloves garlic, minced or pressed**

   1   **tablespoon minced fresh ginger**

   1   **small head baby bok choy, trimmed and thinly sliced (about 1 cup)**

   4   **ounces Chinese pea pods (also called snow peas), ends and strings removed**

   2   **tablespoons dry sherry**

If using shiitake mushrooms, trim off and discard tough stems; then thinly slice shiitake or regular mushrooms. Set aside. In a small bowl, stir together broth, soy sauce, sugar, and vinegar. Set aside.

Toast sesame seeds in a wide frying pan or wok over medium heat until golden (about 4 minutes), shaking pan often. Pour out seeds and set aside.

In a 5- to 6-quart pan, cook capellini in about 3 quarts boiling water until just tender to bite (about 5 minutes).

Meanwhile, place pan used to toast sesame seeds over high heat; add oil and ham. Cook, stirring, until ham is lightly browned (about 2 minutes). Remove ham with a slotted spoon and set aside. Add garlic and ginger to pan and cook, stirring, until fragrant (about 30 seconds). Add mushrooms, bok choy, pea pods, and sherry. Cook, stirring, until pea pods are bright green and tender-crisp to bite (about 2 minutes). Pour in broth mixture and bring to a boil. Remove from heat.

Drain pasta well. Add drained pasta to vegetables, then add ham and mix lightly, using 2 forks. Divide pasta between 2 warm plates and offer sesame seeds to sprinkle over each serving. Makes 2 servings.

Per serving: 727 calories, 27 g protein, 99 g carbohydrates, 23 g total fat, 17 mg cholesterol, 1,347 mg sodium

*Asian-style Pasta Primavera (recipe on facing page) sets the stage
for a relaxing dinner. Just stir-fry slivered ham and a trio of fresh vegetables,
mix with slender capellini, and top with a shower of sesame seeds
for a quick, beautiful main dish.*

31

Linguine with Artichokes & Avocados

Preparation time: About 15 minutes

Cooking time: About 15 minutes

Dinner is a celebration of bold flavors when you serve linguine sauced with garlic, onion, ripe olives, and artichoke hearts. Mild, velvety-smooth avocado slices, arranged atop each portion, offer a pleasing contrast to the robust pasta. Sip glasses of white wine with the meal; finish with your favorite fruit dessert.

    2 tablespoons butter or margarine
    1 large clove garlic, minced or pressed
    1 small onion, chopped
    2 ounces mushrooms, thinly sliced
    1 medium-size tomato, peeled, seeded,
       and diced
    2 tablespoons sliced ripe olives
    ½ cup dry white wine
    1 tablespoon lemon juice

    1 jar (about 6 oz.) marinated artichoke
       hearts, drained and sliced
    1 small avocado
    6 ounces dry linguine
       Grated Parmesan cheese

Melt butter in a wide frying pan over medium heat. Add garlic, onion, and mushrooms; cook, stirring occasionally, until mushrooms are soft (about 10 minutes). Stir in tomato, olives, wine, lemon juice, and artichokes. Bring to a boil; boil until reduced by about a third (about 5 minutes).

While sauce is cooking, pit avocado; then peel, slice, and set aside. Also, in a 5- to 6-quart pan, cook linguine in about 3 quarts boiling water until just tender to bite (about 9 minutes).

Drain pasta well, place in a warm bowl, and top with sauce; mix well, using 2 forks. Divide between 2 warm plates and top with avocado. Offer cheese to add to taste. Makes 2 servings.

Per serving: 661 calories, 16 g protein, 83 g carbohydrates, 32 g total fat, 31 mg cholesterol, 653 mg sodium

Penne with Pesto

Preparation time: About 20 minutes

Cooking time: About 9 minutes

A pasta classic can never be improved—or can it? Our traditional pesto is made with fresh basil, garlic, pine nuts, Parmesan, and lots of olive oil; the lowfat version eliminates the nuts and replaces most of the oil with chicken broth for an equally delicious, but much leaner, result. Serve either pesto on your choice of pasta, then follow up with Poached Fish with Fennel & Tomato (page 59).

       Classic Pesto or Lowfat Pesto (recipes follow)
    6 ounces penne, fusilli (corkscrews), or other
       dry pasta shapes
       Basil sprigs (optional)

Prepare Classic Pesto or Lowfat Pesto; set aside.

In a 5- to 6-quart pan, cook penne in about 3 quarts boiling water until just tender to bite (about 9 minutes). Drain pasta, place in a warm bowl, add pesto, and mix well. Divide between 2 warm plates; garnish with basil sprigs, if desired. Makes 2 servings.

Classic Pesto. In a food processor or blender, combine 1 cup chopped **fresh basil;** 2 ounces **Parmesan cheese,** grated; 2 tablespoons **pine nuts;** and 2 cloves **garlic.** Whirl until basil is very finely chopped. With motor running, pour in ¼ cup **olive oil** in a thin stream; continue to whirl until smoothly puréed.

Lowfat Pesto. In a blender or food processor, combine 1 cup chopped **fresh basil;** 2 ounces **Parmesan cheese,** grated; 2 cloves **garlic;** and 1 tablespoon **olive oil.** Whirl until basil is very finely chopped. With motor running, pour in ¼ cup cold **chicken broth** in a thin stream; continue to whirl until smoothly puréed.

Per serving with Classic Pesto: 757 calories, 26 g protein, 72 g carbohydrates, 42 g total fat, 22 mg cholesterol, 538 mg sodium

Per serving with Lowfat Pesto: 535 calories, 24 g protein, 71 g carbohydrates, 17 g total fat, 22 mg cholesterol, 661 mg sodium

Vermicelli with Chicory

Preparation time: About 15 minutes

Cooking time: About 11 minutes

Nippy and tart when raw, the greens of the chicory family (including curly endive, escarole, radicchio, and Belgian endive) take on a mellow flavor when cooked. Here, the shredded leaves are combined with pancetta and vermicelli for a savory first course. To keep up the "green" theme, choose Spinach-stuffed Game Hens (page 51) as your entrée.

- 6 **ounces dry vermicelli**
- 2 **slices pancetta or bacon (about 2 oz. *total*), chopped**
- 2 **green onions, thinly sliced**
- 3 **parsley sprigs**
- ¾ **cup chicken broth**
- 1 **teaspoon grated lemon peel**
- 6 **cups lightly packed shredded curly endive, escarole, radicchio, or Belgian endive, rinsed and drained**
- 1 **tablespoon lemon juice (if using radicchio)**

Salt and pepper
Grated Parmesan cheese

In a 5- to 6-quart pan, cook vermicelli in about 3 quarts boiling water until just tender to bite (about 9 minutes). Drain well, pour into a warm bowl, and keep warm.

While pasta is cooking, cook pancetta in a wide frying pan over medium-high heat until lightly browned (about 4 minutes), stirring. Add onions and parsley and cook, stirring, until onions are limp (about 1 minute). Add broth and lemon peel. Bring to a boil; boil until liquid is reduced by about a third (about 3 minutes). Remove and discard parsley. Stir in endive or other greens (and lemon juice, if using radicchio) and cook, stirring, until greens are wilted (about 3 minutes).

Add endive mixture to pasta and mix lightly, using 2 forks. Season to taste with salt and pepper and divide between 2 warm plates. Offer cheese to add to taste. Makes 2 servings.

Per serving: 515 calories, 17 g protein, 70 g carbohydrates, 18 g total fat, 19 mg cholesterol, 606 mg sodium

Bucatini, Amatrice Style

Preparation time: About 15 minutes

Cooking time: About 20 minutes

The smokiness of pancetta and the kick of hot red pepper enliven this simple tomato sauce, a specialty from Amatrice (a small town in central Italy). The sauce is traditionally served over long, hollow noodles known as *bucatini*, but spaghetti or linguine does just as well. Add chianti, a green salad, and crusty bread for a classic Italian feast.

- 4 **slices pancetta or bacon (about 4 oz. *total*), chopped**
- 1 **medium-size onion, chopped**
- ½ **teaspoon crushed red pepper flakes**
- 1 **can (about 14½ oz.) pear-shaped tomatoes**
- 1 **clove garlic, minced or pressed**
- ⅓ **cup dry white wine**
- 2 **tablespoons chopped parsley**

- 8 **ounces bucatini or other dry pasta strands**
  Grated Parmesan cheese

Cook pancetta in a wide frying pan over medium-high heat until crisp (about 5 minutes), stirring. Lift out with a slotted spoon, drain, and set aside.

Add onion and pepper flakes to drippings in pan. Cook, stirring, until onion is soft (about 5 minutes). Cut up tomatoes; add tomatoes and their liquid, garlic, wine, and parsley to pan. Bring to a boil; then reduce heat and simmer until slightly thickened (about 10 minutes), stirring occasionally.

Meanwhile, in a 5- to 6-quart pan, cook bucatini in about 3 quarts boiling water until just tender to bite (about 10 minutes). Drain well and place in a warm bowl.

Mix pancetta into sauce; spoon over pasta. Mix well, using 2 forks. Divide between 2 warm plates; offer cheese to add to taste. Makes 2 servings.

Per serving: 822 calories, 22 g protein, 98 g carbohydrates, 35 g total fat, 38 mg cholesterol, 736 mg sodium

*Make tonight's pasta dish a delicious surprise: cook tiny orzo
with broth and vegetables, then enrich the mixture with Parmesan cheese.
Impressive on its own as a first course, Pasta Risotto with Asparagus (recipe
on facing page) also goes well with juicy veal chops and braised
red Swiss chard.*

Pasta Risotto with Asparagus

Preparation time: About 10 minutes

Cooking time: 12 to 15 minutes

This delicious first course or side dish will remind you of classic *risotto*—but it's made with tiny pasta shapes, not rice. You cook the pasta gently in chicken broth, then add sliced fresh asparagus and Parmesan cheese. The result is worthy of a special main course, such as broiled veal chops with braised Swiss chard.

  1 **cup orzo (rice-shaped pasta) or other tiny pasta shapes, such as stars or letters**

1½ **cups *each* chicken broth and water**

  2 **cups 1-inch-long asparagus pieces**
     About ¼ cup grated Parmesan cheese

In a 2- to 3-quart pan, combine pasta, broth, and water. Bring to a boil over high heat; then reduce heat and simmer gently for 5 minutes. Add asparagus and continue to simmer until pasta has absorbed almost all liquid and mixture is like a thick soup (7 to 10 more minutes); stir often to prevent sticking.

Stir ¼ cup of the cheese into pasta mixture, then divide between 2 warm plates. Offer additional cheese to add to taste, if desired. Makes 2 servings.

Per serving: 466 calories, 23 g protein, 80 g carbohydrates, 6 g total fat, 8 mg cholesterol, 936 mg sodium

Seashells with Cauliflower Sauce

Preparation time: About 15 minutes

Cooking time: About 14 minutes

Here's an innovative way to use one of nature's most nutritious vegetables. Cut cauliflower into chunks, cook it briefly, and combine it with pasta shells in a thick tomato purée. The dish makes a nice light supper on its own, and it's just as good as an accompaniment to Garlic-Lemon Red Snapper (page 56).

  2 **tablespoons olive oil**
 ¼ **teaspoon dry thyme**
  1 **medium-size onion, thinly sliced**
  1 **medium-size carrot, finely chopped**
  1 **clove garlic, minced or pressed**
 ½ **cup dry white wine**
  1 **can (about 14½ oz.) pear-shaped tomatoes**
  8 **ounces shell-shaped pasta**
1½ **cups coarsely chopped cauliflower**
     Freshly ground pepper
     Chopped parsley
     Grated Parmesan cheese

Heat oil in a wide frying pan over medium-high heat. Add thyme, onion, and carrot; cook, stirring often, until onion is soft and golden (about 7 minutes). Stir in garlic and wine; bring to a boil. Cut up tomatoes; add tomatoes and their liquid to pan. Bring to a boil, then reduce heat and simmer, stirring occasionally, until juices are thickened (about 7 minutes). Remove sauce from heat, pour into a food processor or blender, and whirl until puréed. Set aside.

While sauce is simmering, in a 5- to 6-quart pan, cook pasta in about 3 quarts boiling water for 5 minutes. Add cauliflower, stir well, and continue to boil until pasta is just tender to bite (about 5 more minutes). Drain pasta and cauliflower well, then return to pan and pour in tomato sauce. Mix lightly; season to taste with pepper. Divide pasta mixture between 2 warm shallow bowls and sprinkle with parsley; offer cheese to add to taste. Makes 2 servings.

Per serving: 633 calories, 19 g protein, 105 g carbohydrates, 16 g total fat, 0 mg cholesterol, 371 mg sodium

Fettuccine with Spicy Chicken & Vegetables

Preparation time: About 15 minutes

Cooking time: About 17 minutes

If you enjoy Mediterranean flavors, you'll want to try this well-seasoned combination of chicken and vegetables, served over fresh spinach pasta and topped with toasted pine nuts. The dish is easily hearty enough for a whole meal, but if appetites demand, precede the pasta with an Italian-style first course—perhaps Avocado, Zucchini & Arugula Salad (page 28).

- ¼ cup pine nuts
- 2 tablespoons olive oil
- 1 small onion, finely chopped
- 2 cloves garlic, minced or pressed
- ¾ teaspoon *each* dry basil and dry oregano
- ¼ teaspoon crushed red pepper flakes
- 1 boneless, skinless chicken breast half (about 4 oz.), cut into ½-inch cubes
- 1 small zucchini, thinly sliced
- 4 ounces mushrooms, sliced
- 1 large tomato, chopped
- 8 ounces fresh spinach fettuccine
- ¼ cup grated Parmesan cheese

Toast pine nuts in a small frying pan over medium heat until golden (about 4 minutes), stirring often. Set aside.

Heat oil in a wide frying pan over medium-high heat. Add onion, garlic, basil, oregano, and pepper flakes. Cook, stirring often, until onion is soft (about 5 minutes). Add chicken, zucchini, mushrooms, and tomato. Cook, stirring, until mushrooms are soft and chicken is no longer pink in center; cut to test (about 5 minutes). Remove from heat and keep warm.

In a 5- to 6-quart pan, cook fettuccine in about 3 quarts boiling water until just tender to bite (about 3 minutes). Drain well and place in a warm bowl; spoon chicken sauce over pasta and mix lightly, using 2 forks. Divide between 2 warm plates; sprinkle with pine nuts and cheese. Makes 2 servings.

Per serving: 700 calories, 41 g protein, 71 g carbohydrates, 31 g total fat, 170 mg cholesterol, 328 mg sodium

Pictured on page 95

Spinach Pasta & Salmon in Champagne Cream Sauce

Preparation time: About 15 minutes

Cooking time: About 17 minutes

Save this rich pasta treat for a special night when romance is on the menu. Start the meal with oysters on the half shell, then bring on plates of green noodles and poached fresh salmon in a creamy sauce. For dessert, you might choose Fresh Fruit in Lemon-Ginger Syrup (page 75).

- 1 cup brut champagne
- 2 cups water
- ½ teaspoon whole allspice
- 1 bay leaf
- 8 ounces salmon fillet (¾ to 1 inch thick)
- 1¼ cups whipping cream
- 6 ounces dry spinach egg noodles
- 2 tablespoons butter or margarine
- ¼ cup 2-inch-long chive strips or ¼ cup thinly sliced green onions

In a wide frying pan, combine champagne, water, allspice, and bay leaf. Bring to a boil over high heat. Add salmon, reduce heat, cover, and simmer until just opaque but still moist in thickest part; cut to test (about 7 minutes). Lift out salmon, reserving poaching liquid. Carefully remove and discard skin and any bones from salmon, then break flesh into bite-size pieces. Set aside.

Pour poaching liquid through a fine strainer into a bowl; discard seasonings. Return liquid to frying pan and add cream. Bring to a boil; boil, stirring occasionally, until reduced to 1¼ cups (about 10 minutes). Keep warm over lowest heat.

Meanwhile, in a 5- to 6-quart pan, cook noodles in about 3 quarts boiling water until just tender to bite (about 5 minutes). Drain noodles; add noodles and butter to cream mixture, then add salmon. Mix lightly, using 2 forks. Divide between 2 warm plates and sprinkle with chives. Makes 2 servings.

Per serving: 1,032 calories, 39 g protein, 66 g carbohydrates, 69 g total fat, 340 mg cholesterol, 286 mg sodium

Italian Stir-fried Pasta with Shrimp

Preparation time: About 15 minutes

Cooking time: About 9 minutes

This quick-to-fix dinner combines two culinary classics—an Asian stir-fry and Italian pasta. Have all the ingredients prepared and at the ready before you start to cook; once the stir-frying starts, it goes very quickly. To accompany the colorful main dish, try Parmesan Toast (page 44) and a salad of sliced tomatoes and red onions.

- 6 ounces dry linguine or other thin dry pasta strands
- 2 tablespoons olive oil
- 1 small onion, cut into bite-size chunks
- 1 medium-size green bell pepper, seeded and cut into bite-size chunks
- ¼ teaspoon crushed red pepper flakes
- 1 teaspoon dry oregano
- 2 ounces Chinese pea pods (also called snow peas), ends and strings removed
- 1 tablespoon butter or margarine
- 12 ounces small cooked shrimp
  Grated Parmesan cheese

In a 5- to 6-quart pan, cook pasta in about 3 quarts boiling water until just tender to bite (about 9 minutes).

Meanwhile, heat oil in a wok or wide frying pan over high heat. Add onion, bell pepper, pepper flakes, and oregano. Cook, stirring, until vegetables are tender-crisp to bite (about 4 minutes). Add pea pods and butter; continue to cook, stirring, until pea pods turn bright green (about 2 more minutes). Add shrimp, stir well, and remove pan from heat.

Drain pasta well, place in a warm bowl, and top with shrimp mixture; mix lightly, using 2 forks. Divide between 2 warm shallow bowls or plates and offer cheese to add to taste. Makes 2 servings.

Per serving: 685 calories, 48 g protein, 70 g carbohydrates, 23 g total fat, 347 mg cholesterol, 448 mg sodium

Fettuccine with Crab

Preparation time: About 15 minutes

Cooking time: About 9 minutes

Aficionados of fresh crab will adore this simple pasta. Tossed with green onions, diced fresh tomatoes, and fettuccine, just half a pound of crabmeat makes a satisfying dinner for two. Offer Fennel Salad with Oranges (page 29) alongside.

- 6 ounces dry fettuccine
- 2 tablespoons butter or margarine
- 2 tablespoons olive oil
- ½ cup thinly sliced green onions
- 1 clove garlic, minced or pressed
- 2 medium-size tomatoes, peeled, seeded, and chopped
- ¼ cup dry white wine
- 1 tablespoon lemon juice
- 8 ounces cooked crabmeat
- ¼ cup finely chopped parsley
  Salt and pepper

In a 5- to 6-quart pan, cook fettuccine in about 3 quarts boiling water until just tender to bite (about 9 minutes).

Meanwhile, melt butter in oil in a wide frying pan over medium heat. Add onions, garlic, tomatoes, and wine. Bring to a boil, stirring often; then boil until tomatoes are softened (about 5 minutes). Add lemon juice, crab, and parsley. Stir gently just until crab is heated through (about 2 minutes). Season to taste with salt and pepper.

Drain pasta well, place in a warm bowl, and top with crab sauce; mix lightly, using 2 forks. Divide between 2 warm plates. Makes 2 servings.

Per serving: 698 calories, 37 g protein, 69 g carbohydrates, 31 g total fat, 225 mg cholesterol, 468 mg sodium

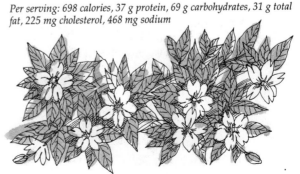

Succulent Meats & Poultry

Pictured on facing page

Grilled Steak with Grilled Tomato Relish

Preparation time: About 15 minutes

Grilling time: About 15 minutes

Dinner from the barbecue is twice as tantalizing when you cook an aromatic tomato relish on the grill right alongside a show-stopping steak. If you like, rub a few slices of crusty bread with olive oil and grill them, too.

- 1 **bone-in beefsteak such as T-bone or porterhouse (about 1¼ lbs.), trimmed of excess fat**
- 3 **medium-size pear-shaped tomatoes, cut in half lengthwise**
- 2 **tablespoons olive oil**
- 1 **medium-size onion, chopped**
- 1 **clove garlic, minced or pressed**
- ¼ **cup chopped fresh basil or 2 tablespoons dry basil**
  Salt and pepper
  Basil sprigs (optional)

Place steak on a lightly greased grill 4 to 6 inches above a solid bed of medium-hot coals. Cook, turning as needed, until evenly browned on outside and done to your liking; cut to test (about 15 minutes for medium-rare).

Meanwhile, place tomatoes, cut sides up, on grill and brush lightly with 1 tablespoon of the oil. When tomatoes are browned on bottom (about 3 minutes), turn over and continue to cook until soft when pressed (about 3 more minutes).

While tomatoes are grilling, combine remaining 1 tablespoon oil, onion, and garlic in a medium-size frying pan with a heatproof handle. Set pan over coals (or set on the range over medium-high heat). Cook, stirring often, until onion is limp and golden (about 10 minutes); stir in chopped basil.

When tomatoes are soft, stir them into onion mixture, then set pan aside on a cooler area of grill (or cover and keep warm on range).

When steak is done, place it on a board with a well (or on a platter); spoon tomato relish alongside steak. Season to taste with salt and pepper and garnish with basil sprigs, if desired. To serve, carve meat away from bone, then cut it into thin slices. Spoon accumulated meat juices into tomato relish, if desired. Makes 2 servings.

Per serving: 449 calories, 38 g protein, 14 g carbohydrates, 27 g total fat, 100 mg cholesterol, 100 mg sodium

Fire up the barbecue for a feast sure to delight dedicated beef-eaters. Grilled Steak with Grilled Tomato Relish (recipe on facing page) pairs a tender T-bone with a topping of basil-seasoned onions and fresh tomatoes. Cool red wine sangria is great with this hearty menu.

39

Cabbage-Paprika Stroganoff

Preparation time: About 15 minutes

Cooking time: About 40 minutes

Shredded cabbage adds vitamins, fiber, and flavor to this hearty classic; yogurt makes the creamy sauce lower in fat. To complete a stout supper, serve steamed carrots and glasses of dark beer.

- 3 slices bacon (about 3 oz. *total*), chopped
- 12 ounces boneless top round or sirloin tip steak, trimmed of excess fat and cut across the grain into ¼-inch-thick slices
- 1 medium-size onion, thinly sliced
- ½ small head green cabbage, coarsely shredded
- 1 tablespoon paprika
- ½ cup *each* sour cream and plain lowfat yogurt
  Hot cooked egg noodles
- 2 teaspoons minced parsley

Cook bacon in a wide frying pan over medium heat until crisp (about 5 minutes), stirring often. Lift out with a slotted spoon, drain, and set aside. Pour off and discard all but 2 tablespoons of the drippings from pan.

Increase heat to high and add beef to drippings in pan; cook, stirring, just until browned (about 4 minutes). With a slotted spoon, transfer beef to a small bowl; set aside. To pan, add onion, cabbage, and paprika; cook, stirring, until cabbage is limp (about 4 minutes). Reduce heat, cover, and simmer until cabbage is very soft (about 25 minutes).

Return beef to pan; heat through (about 2 minutes). Stir sour cream and yogurt into beef mixture; cook just until hot (do not boil). Spoon noodles onto 2 dinner plates, top with stroganoff, and sprinkle with bacon and parsley. Makes 2 servings.

Per serving: 587 calories, 50 g protein, 18 g carbohydrates, 35 g total fat, 145 mg cholesterol, 436 mg sodium

Sweet & Sour Corn Relish Burgers

Preparation time: About 20 minutes

Grilling time: 5 to 10 minutes

Add a novel touch to the familiar hamburger: replace the usual lettuce with crisp spinach leaves and top the meat with a lively homemade corn relish. To use up any leftover fresh spinach, you might serve Mediterranean Spinach (page 64) with the burgers.

- Corn Relish (recipe follows)
- ⅔ pound lean ground beef
- 2 hamburger buns
  Butter or margarine, at room temperature
- 1 cup lightly packed stemmed spinach leaves, rinsed and crisped
- 2 thin slices onion
  Salt and pepper

Prepare Corn Relish and set aside.

Divide beef in half; shape each half into a ½-inch-thick patty. Place patties on a lightly greased grill 4 to 6 inches above a solid bed of hot coals (or place on rack of a broiler pan; broil 3 to 4 inches below heat). Cook, turning once, until patties are browned on outside and done to your liking; cut to test (about 5 minutes for rare, 10 minutes for medium).

While burgers are cooking, spread cut sides of buns lightly with butter. Shortly before burgers are done, place buns, buttered sides down, on a cooler area of grill and cook until lightly toasted (about 2 minutes). Or place buns, buttered sides up, on broiler rack; broil until toasted (about 1 minute).

Arrange spinach leaves equally on bottom halves of buns; then top each bun with a hamburger, an onion slice, and half the Corn Relish. Season to taste with salt and pepper. Cover with top halves of buns. Makes 2 servings.

Corn Relish. In a small bowl, stir together ½ cup **cooked corn kernels;** 1 small **pear-shaped tomato,** diced; 2 tablespoons minced **sweet pickle;** 1 tablespoon *each* **vinegar** and **salad oil;** ½ teaspoon **mustard seeds;** and ¼ teaspoon **pepper.**

Per serving: 563 calories, 33 g protein, 41 g carbohydrates, 30 g total fat, 96 mg cholesterol, 431 mg sodium

Danish Beef Sandwiches

Preparation time: About 20 minutes

Cooking time (for onions): About 6 minutes

Who says dinner can't be a holiday? Offer these open-faced roast beef sandwiches topped with crispy onion rings and feel like you're picnicking in Denmark. Your favorite potato salad is the perfect accompaniment.

Crisp-fried Onions (recipe follows)

1 **tablespoon reduced-calorie or regular mayonnaise**

½ **teaspoon** *each* **prepared horseradish and coarse-grained mustard**

2 **slices pumpernickel or dark rye bread,** *each* **about 4 by 5 inches**

4 **large butter lettuce leaves, rinsed and crisped**
   About 4 ounces thinly sliced rare roast beef
   Salt

Prepare Crisp-fried Onions and keep warm.

Spoon half each of the mayonnaise, horseradish, and mustard onto each slice of bread; then spread condiments over bread to mix. Top each slice with 2 lettuce leaves, then pile beef on lettuce. Mound as many Crisp-fried Onions as you can onto beef; accompany sandwiches with remaining onions and season to taste with salt. Eat sandwiches with a knife and fork. Makes 2 servings.

Crisp-fried Onions. Thinly slice 1 medium-size **onion** and separate into rings. Place 3 tablespoons **all-purpose flour** in a plastic or paper bag. Add onion slices and shake to coat evenly with flour.

In a deep 2½- to 3-quart pan, heat about 1½ inches **salad oil** to 300°F on a deep-frying thermometer. Lift half the onion slices from bag, shake off excess flour, and drop into oil. Cook until onions are golden and sizzling has almost stopped (about 3 minutes); adjust heat to maintain temperature at 300°F. Lift onions from pan with a slotted spoon and drain on paper towels. Repeat to cook remaining onions.

Per serving: 385 calories, 21 g protein, 30 g carbohydrates, 20 g total fat, 49 mg cholesterol, 275 mg sodium

Pork Chops in Sake Marinade

Preparation time: About 10 minutes

Marinating time: At least 2 hours

Cooking time: About 1 hour

An Oriental-style marinade doubles as a delectable sauce for these braised pork chops. Serve with steamed broccoli spears and a rice pilaf brightened up with diced cooked onions, carrots, and celery.

2 **shoulder pork chops (about 6 oz.** *each***), trimmed of excess fat**

1 **cup sake or dry white wine**

¼ **cup thinly sliced green onions**

2 **tablespoons chopped fresh ginger**

1 **tablespoon soy sauce**

1 **clove garlic, minced or pressed**

1 **tablespoon Oriental sesame oil**

Select a shallow dish just large enough to hold pork chops in a single layer. In dish, stir together sake, onions, ginger, soy sauce, and garlic. Lay chops in marinade; cover and refrigerate for at least 2 hours or until next day, turning chops over occasionally.

Heat oil in a medium-size frying pan over medium-high heat. Lift chops from marinade, scraping any onions and ginger back into dish. Cook chops, turning once, until browned on both sides (about 7 minutes). Pour marinade into pan; bring to a boil. Reduce heat, cover, and simmer, turning chops occasionally, until meat is tender when pierced (about 50 minutes). Transfer chops to 2 dinner plates; keep warm.

Boil pan juices over high heat until reduced by half (about 5 minutes). Spoon over chops. Makes 2 servings.

Per serving: 270 calories, 25 g protein, 4 g carbohydrates, 17 g total fat, 83 mg cholesterol, 616 mg sodium

If you love combinations of meat and fruit, you won't want to miss Mustard-glazed Veal Strips (recipe on facing page). Coated in a gingery sweet-sour sauce and baked until fork-tender, the meat is served hot atop a bed of crisp watercress; avocado and papaya slices provide smooth contrast.

Pictured on facing page

Mustard-glazed Veal Strips

Preparation time: About 25 minutes

Cooking time: About 1 hour

Tender veal strips in a tangy-sweet mustard glaze top a cool base of fruit and greens for this refreshing feast. Crusty rolls and a crisp white wine are superb partners for the entrée.

- 1 tablespoon salad oil
- 12 ounces boneless veal stew meat, cut across the grain into ¼-inch-thick strips
  About ¼ cup chicken broth
  Mustard Sauce (recipe follows)
- 1 small ripe avocado
- 2 tablespoons lemon juice
- ½ medium-size ripe papaya
- 1½ cups lightly packed watercress sprigs, rinsed and crisped
  Lemon wedges

Heat oil in a medium-size frying pan over high heat; add veal and cook, stirring, until lightly browned (about 4 minutes). Transfer veal to a 1½- to 2-quart baking dish with a lid. To pan, add ¼ cup of the broth; reduce heat to medium and stir to scrape up browned bits. Pour liquid over veal.

Prepare Mustard Sauce, add to veal, and stir well. Cover dish and bake in a 325° oven for 45 minutes. Uncover; continue to bake, stirring once or twice, until veal is very tender when pierced (about 15 more minutes). Add a few tablespoons more broth if meat begins to dry out.

Just before serving, pit avocado; peel, slice, and coat with lemon juice. Peel, seed, and slice papaya.

Divide watercress between 2 dinner plates; fan out avocado and papaya alongside. Spoon veal mixture over watercress; offer lemon wedges to squeeze over meat and fruit. Makes 2 servings.

Mustard Sauce. In a bowl, stir together 1 small **onion**, finely chopped; 2 tablespoons **Dijon mustard**; 1½ tablespoons **honey**; 1 tablespoon **soy sauce**; 1 tablespoon **raspberry or red wine vinegar**; 2 teaspoons chopped **fresh rosemary** or 1 teaspoon dry rosemary; 1 tablespoon finely chopped **fresh ginger**; and ½ teaspoon coarsely ground **pepper**.

Per serving: 522 calories, 37 g protein, 31 g carbohydrates, 29 g total fat, 139 mg cholesterol, 1,255 mg sodium

Pictured on page 66

Veal Patties with Marsala Sauce

Preparation time: About 15 minutes

Cooking time: About 10 minutes

These thyme-seasoned veal patties are wrapped in bacon, broiled, and served with a savory mushroom-wine sauce. For side dishes, you might choose mashed potatoes and cooked baby carrots.

- ⅔ pound lean ground veal
- 1 teaspoon dry thyme
  Salt and pepper
- 2 slices bacon (about 2 oz. *total*)
- 1 tablespoon butter or margarine
- ⅓ pound mushrooms, sliced
- 2 green onions, thinly sliced
- ¼ cup marsala or dry sherry
- ¼ cup chicken broth
- 1 teaspoon cornstarch

In a bowl, mix veal and thyme; season to taste with salt and pepper. Divide mixture in half; shape each half into a ¾-inch-thick patty. Drape a slice of bacon over each patty, tucking ends together beneath patty. Place patties on rack of a broiler pan. Broil about 4 inches below heat, turning once, until bacon is browned and veal is done to your liking; cut to test (about 10 minutes for medium).

Meanwhile, melt butter in a medium-size frying pan over medium-high heat. Add mushrooms and onions; cook, stirring, until mushrooms are soft and lightly browned (about 7 minutes). Pour in marsala, bring to a boil, and boil for 1 minute. Stir together broth and cornstarch, add to pan, and stir until sauce boils and thickens (about 1 minute); season to taste with salt and pepper.

Place veal patties on 2 dinner plates and top with sauce. Makes 2 servings.

Per serving: 316 calories, 29 g protein, 10 g carbohydrates, 18 g total fat, 125 mg cholesterol, 398 mg sodium

Better Bread & Vinaigrettes

When you're cooking for two, you usually want to keep the menu simple: focusing on just one recipe means less planning, less preparation, and less cleanup. But if you want to offer more than a pasta, soup, or meat main dish, what do you offer to complete the meal? The easiest choice is often bread or green salad (or both); few other side dishes are as simple or as suitable with so many entrées. Unfortunately, though, these tried-and-true accompaniments can become a bit redundant. Below, we offer four ways to make standard bread and salad more interesting.

Parmesan-sprinkled toast and garlicky herbed batons can be dunked into your favorite soups, served with whole-meal salads, or offered as fillers alongside meat, chicken, and fish. Our foolproof vinaigrettes—one seasoned with tangy mustard, the other with minced fresh herbs—are equally good on wedges of mild iceberg lettuce, a potpourri of flavorful field greens, or blanched seasonal vegetables.

Parmesan Toast

In a small bowl, beat together ¼ cup **butter** or margarine (at room temperature) and ½ cup grated **Parmesan cheese.** Cut 1 small **baguette** (about 4 oz.) into ½-inch-thick slanting slices. Spread butter mixture over one side of each slice. Arrange slices, buttered sides up, on a baking sheet. Broil about 4 inches below heat until golden (about 4 minutes). Makes 2 servings.

Per serving: 459 calories, 14 g protein, 32 g carbohydrates, 31 g total fat, 80 mg cholesterol, 935 mg sodium

Giant Herbed Breadsticks

In a small bowl, beat together ¼ cup **butter** or margarine (at room temperature); ¼ cup minced **green onions;** ¼ teaspoon **dry thyme;** and 1 clove **garlic,** minced or pressed. Cut 1 small **baguette** (about 4 oz.) lengthwise into quarters. Spread

butter mixture over cut sides of bread. Arrange bread on a baking sheet; broil about 4 inches below heat until golden (about 4 minutes). Makes 2 servings.

Per serving: 374 calories, 6 g protein, 33 g carbohydrates, 25 g total fat, 64 mg cholesterol, 564 mg sodium

Herb Vinaigrette

In a small bowl, whisk together 3 tablespoons **olive oil,** 3 tablespoons **balsamic or red wine vinegar,** 2 tablespoons snipped **chives** or minced green onion, and 1 teaspoon chopped **fresh oregano** or 1 teaspoon dry oregano. Makes about ⅓ cup.

Per tablespoon: 74 calories, 0.1 g protein, 0.5 g carbohydrates, 8 g total fat, 0 mg cholesterol, 0.1 mg sodium

Dijon Vinaigrette

In a small bowl, whisk together 2 tablespoons **red wine vinegar** and ½ teaspoon **Dijon mustard** until smooth. Add ¼ cup **extra-virgin olive oil;** whisk until smooth. Season to taste with **salt** and freshly ground **pepper.** Makes about ⅓ cup.

Per tablespoon: 97 calories, 0 g protein, .26 g carbohydrates, 11 g total fat, 0 mg cholesterol, 15 mg sodium

Lamb Shanks with Hominy & Mint Aïoli

Preparation time: About 20 minutes

Cooking time: About 3 hours

A single dry red chile adds mild heat to a slow-cooked lamb stew you serve with cool mint mayonnaise. Spoon the meat and vegetables over noodles; offer kale alongside.

- 2 **tablespoons salad oil**
- 2 **lamb shanks (about 1 lb. *each*), bones cracked**
- 1 **red bell pepper, seeded and thinly sliced**
- 1 **large onion, thinly sliced**
- 1 **clove garlic, minced or pressed**
- 1 **cup chicken broth**
- 1 **dry California (Anaheim) or New Mexico chile, stemmed, seeded, and rinsed; or 1 teaspoon chili powder**
- 1 **can (about 1 lb.) white or yellow hominy**
  Mint Aïoli (recipe follows)

Heat 1 tablespoon of the oil in a deep 10- to 12-inch frying pan over medium-high heat. Add lamb and cook, turning often, until browned on all sides (about 10 minutes). Lift out lamb; set aside. Add bell pepper and cook, stirring often, until limp (about 5 minutes). Remove from pan and set aside.

Heat remaining 1 tablespoon oil in pan; add onion and garlic. Stir until onion is golden (about 7 minutes). Return lamb to pan. Add broth and chile; bring to a boil. Reduce heat to very low, cover, and simmer for 1½ hours. Turn lamb over; drain hominy and add to pan. Cover; continue to simmer until lamb is very tender when pierced (about 1 more hour). Meanwhile, prepare Mint Aïoli.

Lift lamb from pan. Add bell pepper to pan, then bring mixture to a boil over high heat; pour over lamb. Discard chile, if desired. Offer Mint Aïoli to add to each serving. Makes 2 servings.

Per serving without Mint Aïoli: 973 calories, 64 g protein, 45 g carbohydrates, 59 g total fat, 202 mg cholesterol, 1,042 mg sodium

Mint Aïoli. Mix 1 clove **garlic,** pressed; 2 tablespoons finely minced **fresh mint;** and ¼ cup **mayonnaise.** Cover and refrigerate. Makes ⅓ cup.

Per tablespoon: 80 calories, 0.2 g protein, 0.5 g carbohydrates, 9 g total fat, 6 mg cholesterol, 63 mg sodium

Lamb Moussaka

Preparation time: About 20 minutes

Cooking time: About 45 minutes

To accompany this delicious family-style casserole, serve sliced cucumbers tossed with plain yogurt, vinegar, and dill.

- 1 **large eggplant (about 1¼ lbs.)**
- 3 **tablespoons salad oil**
- 1 **medium-size onion, chopped**
- 8 **ounces lean ground lamb or beef**
- 1 **small can (about 8 oz.) tomato sauce**
- 1 **tablespoon chopped parsley**
- ½ **teaspoon *each* dry thyme and ground cinnamon**
- ½ **cup dry red wine**
- ½ **cup shredded jack or mozzarella cheese**

Cut eggplant crosswise into about ½-inch-thick slices. Brush cut sides of slices with 2 tablespoons of the oil, then arrange in a single layer in a shallow baking pan. Bake in a 425° oven until browned and very soft when pierced (about 25 minutes).

While eggplant is baking, heat remaining 1 tablespoon oil in a wide frying pan over medium-high heat. Add onion and cook, stirring often, until soft (about 5 minutes). Add lamb and cook, stirring often, until crumbly and no longer pink (about 5 minutes). Drain fat from pan, then stir in tomato sauce, parsley, thyme, cinnamon, and wine. Reduce heat and simmer until slightly thickened (about 10 minutes), stirring occasionally.

In a 1½- to 2-quart casserole, arrange half the eggplant. Top with meat mixture, then with remaining eggplant. Sprinkle with cheese and bake in a 375° oven until bubbly at edges and golden on top (about 20 minutes). Makes 2 servings.

Per serving: 622 calories, 31 g protein, 27 g carbohydrates, 45 g total fat, 101 mg cholesterol, 915 mg sodium

Spicy Oven-fried Chicken & Potatoes

Preparation time: About 10 minutes

Baking time: About 45 minutes

Chicken legs and potato wedges baked in a crisp, spicy cornmeal coating are just right for a quick weeknight meal. Serve with sautéed leeks; offer gewürztraminer or mineral water to drink.

- ½ **cup yellow cornmeal**
- 1 **tablespoon all-purpose flour**
- 2 **teaspoons chili powder**
- ½ **teaspoon crushed red pepper flakes**
- 2 **whole chicken legs (about 10 oz. *each*)**
- 2 **tablespoons salad oil**
- 2 **small russet potatoes, scrubbed**

In a wide, shallow bowl, mix cornmeal, flour, chili powder, and pepper flakes. Rinse chicken, pat dry, and brush evenly with 1 tablespoon of the oil. Roll chicken in cornmeal mixture to coat completely. Then place chicken, skin side up, on a rack in a 10- by 15-inch baking pan.

Cut each potato lengthwise into quarters. In a bowl, mix potato quarters with remaining 1 tablespoon oil. Then place potatoes in cornmeal mixture and toss to coat. Arrange potatoes on rack around chicken. Bake in a 400° oven until potatoes are tender when pierced and chicken is crusty on outside and no longer pink near thighbone; cut to test (about 45 minutes). Makes 2 servings.

Per serving: 732 calories, 43 g protein, 62 g carbohydrates, 34 g total fat, 129 mg cholesterol, 161 mg sodium

Pictured on facing page

Grilled Chicken & Vegetables with Sesame Sauce

Preparation time: About 20 minutes

Marinating time: At least 30 minutes

Grilling time: About 30 minutes

Served with a spicy sesame sauce, these grilled marinated vegetables and chicken legs make an easy warm-weather meal. For an Asian-style accompaniment, present steamed short-grain white rice seasoned with rice vinegar.

- 2 **whole chicken legs (about 10 oz. *each*)**
- 4 **large fresh shiitake mushrooms, *each* about 3 inches in diameter; or 4 large fresh regular mushrooms**
- ¼ **cup dry sherry or sake**
- 1 **tablespoon soy sauce**
- 2 **teaspoons Oriental sesame oil**
- 4 **green onions, ends trimmed**
- 2 **small crookneck squash, ends trimmed, cut in half lengthwise**
   Sesame Sauce (recipe follows)

Rinse chicken and pat dry. If using shiitake mushrooms, trim off and discard tough stems.

Stir together sherry, soy sauce, and oil; then pour half the mixture into each of 2 shallow dishes. Place chicken in one dish; place mushrooms, on-ions, and squash in other dish. Cover and refrigerate, turning chicken and vegetables occasionally, for at least 30 minutes or up to 2 hours. Meanwhile, prepare Sesame Sauce and set aside.

Drain chicken, reserving marinade. Place chicken on a lightly greased grill 4 to 6 inches above a solid bed of medium-hot coals. Cook, turning once, for 5 minutes. Lift vegetables from marinade; arrange on grill. Cook, brushing chicken and vegetables occasionally with marinade and turning to brown evenly, until onions and mushrooms are lightly browned (5 to 10 minutes for onions, 10 to 15 minutes for mushrooms), squash is tender when pierced (about 20 minutes), and chicken meat near thighbone is no longer pink; cut to test (about 25 minutes). As each food is done, remove it from grill and keep warm. Serve with Sesame Sauce. Makes 2 servings.

Per serving without Sesame Sauce: 430 calories, 40 g protein, 14 g carbohydrates, 24 g total fat, 129 mg cholesterol, 645 mg sodium

Sesame Sauce. Mix ¼ cup **tahini** (sesame butter); 2 tablespoons **warm water;** 1 tablespoon *each* **lemon juice, soy sauce,** and minced **fresh ginger;** 1½ teaspoons **sugar;** 1 clove **garlic,** pressed; and a pinch of **ground red pepper** (cayenne). Makes ⅓ cup.

Per tablespoon: 81 calories, 2 g protein, 5 g carbohydrates, 6 g total fat, 0 mg cholesterol, 220 mg sodium

Warm weather seems made for outdoor meals like Grilled
Chicken & Vegetables with Sesame Sauce (recipe on facing page). Marinated whole chicken legs, slender green onions, halved summer squash, and
shiitake mushrooms are all cooked together on the barbecue, then topped
with a creamy blend of tahini, soy, and other seasonings. Enjoy chilled
sparkling mineral water alongside the hot meat and vegetables.

47

Tandoori Barbecued Chicken

Preparation time: About 15 minutes

Marinating time: At least 1 hour

Grilling time: About 40 minutes

Traditional tandoori-style foods are baked in a very hot clay oven; to make these robustly flavored chicken legs, we've adapted the recipe for a barbecue or traditional oven. Choose Indian-style accompaniments, such as Barley & Lentils with Mint (page 65) and steamed cauliflower.

 1 tablespoon white wine vinegar
 ¼ cup lime juice
 ½ teaspoon *each* crushed red pepper flakes, cumin seeds, and ground turmeric
 ¾ teaspoon paprika
 2 tablespoons *each* chopped cilantro and parsley
 2 cloves garlic, minced or pressed
 1 tablespoon minced fresh ginger
 ½ cup plain lowfat or nonfat yogurt
 2 whole chicken legs (about 10 oz. *each*)

In a blender or food processor, whirl vinegar, lime juice, pepper flakes, cumin seeds, turmeric, paprika, cilantro, parsley, garlic, and ginger until blended. Add yogurt and whirl until smooth.

Rinse chicken and pat dry. With a sharp knife, slash each chicken leg through to thigh and drumstick bones along entire length. Place chicken in a medium-size bowl; add yogurt marinade and turn chicken to coat well. Cover and refrigerate for at least 1 hour or until next day.

To grill chicken, ignite 30 to 40 charcoal briquets on fire grate of a barbecue with a lid. When coals are dotted with gray ash, bank about half of them on each side of fire grate; place a metal drip pan in center. Set cooking grill in place 4 to 6 inches above coals; lightly grease grill.

Drain chicken briefly, reserving marinade; place chicken on grill above drip pan. Cover barbecue, open drafts, and cook chicken, basting occasionally with marinade, until meat near thighbone is no longer pink; cut to test (about 40 minutes).

To oven-cook chicken, drain briefly, reserving marinade; place chicken in a 7- by 11-inch baking dish. Bake in a 350° oven for 30 minutes, basting occasionally with marinade. Then transfer chicken to a foil-lined broiler rack. Broil 4 to 6 inches below heat, turning once or twice, until skin is crisp and meat neat thighbone is no longer pink; cut to test (about 10 minutes). Makes 2 servings.

Per serving: 383 calories, 40 g protein, 9 g carbohydrates, 20 g total fat, 132 mg cholesterol, 170 mg sodium

Sautéed Chicken Livers with Apples & Onions

Preparation time: About 10 minutes

Cooking time: About 15 minutes

Sautéed apple slices add a sweet, mellow accent to the time-honored duo of liver and onions. For a double dose of hard-to-get iron, spoon cooked spinach alongside.

 8 ounces chicken livers
 2 tablespoons butter or margarine
 1 medium-size onion, thinly sliced
 1 medium-size Golden Delicious apple, peeled, cored, and cut into ¼-inch-thick slices
 ¼ teaspoon dry thyme
 1 tablespoon Worcestershire
 2 English muffins, split and toasted

Rinse chicken livers, pat dry, and set aside.

Melt 1 tablespoon of the butter in a medium-size frying pan over medium-high heat. Add onion and cook, stirring occasionally, until golden (about 7 minutes). Push onion to side of pan and add apple slices. Cook, turning gently, until golden brown and soft when pierced (about 4 minutes). Lift apple and onion from pan; keep warm.

Melt remaining 1 tablespoon butter in pan. Add chicken livers and cook, turning with a spatula, until browned on outside but still slightly pink inside; cut to test (about 4 minutes). Return apple and onion to pan; add thyme and Worcestershire and stir to scrape up browned bits. To serve, spoon over or alongside muffins. Makes 2 servings.

Per serving: 431 calories, 25 g protein, 44 g carbohydrates, 17 g total fat, 529 mg cholesterol, 580 mg sodium

Chicken Pocket Sandwiches

Preparation time: About 15 minutes

Cooking time: About 9 minutes

Here's an ideal hot stuffing for pita breads: stir-fried chicken, ripe olives, spinach, and capers in a garlicky sauce. Add bowls of steaming Broccoli-Buttermilk Soup (page 17), then settle down in front of the TV or a crackling fire for a nourishing cold-weather meal.

- 1 tablespoon butter or margarine
- 1 tablespoon salad oil
- 1 clove garlic, minced or pressed
- ¼ teaspoon crushed red pepper flakes
- 2 boneless, skinless chicken breast halves (about 8 oz. *total*), cut into ½-inch chunks
- ¼ cup dry red wine
- 2 tablespoons *each* chopped parsley and drained capers
- 1 can (about 2¼ oz.) sliced ripe olives, drained
- 2 anchovy fillets, finely chopped (optional)
- 3 cups lightly packed torn spinach leaves, rinsed and drained
  Salt and pepper
- 2 whole wheat pita breads

Melt butter in oil in a wide frying pan or wok over medium-high heat. Add garlic, pepper flakes, and chicken. Cook, stirring, until chicken is opaque on outside (about 3 minutes). Add wine, bring to a boil, and boil until reduced by half (about 1 minute); then stir in parsley, capers, olives, and, if desired, anchovies. Add spinach and continue to cook, stirring, until spinach is wilted and chicken is no longer pink in center; cut to test (about 5 more minutes). Season to taste with salt and pepper.

Slice about a quarter off the top of each pita bread; invert this piece and slide it inside bread, pushing it to bottom (this reinforces bottom of bread, keeping filling from leaking through). Fill each bread with chicken mixture; serve at once. Makes 2 servings.

Per serving: 466 calories, 35 g protein, 42 g carbohydrates, 18 g total fat, 81 mg cholesterol, 1,069 mg sodium

Coq au Vin with Rice

Preparation time: About 15 minutes

Cooking time: About 42 minutes

To make this easy adaptation of a French classic, you simmer rice along with the chicken. The dish can be made with white or red wine; you need only half a cup to flavor the sauce, so serve the rest of the bottle with the meal. Round out the menu with a green vegetable—perhaps buttered green beans with toasted almonds.

- 2 chicken thighs (about 4 oz. *each*)
- 2 slices bacon (about 2 oz. *total*), chopped
- 1 clove garlic, minced or pressed
- 1 medium-size onion, chopped
- 4 ounces mushrooms, sliced
- 1 cup chicken broth
- ½ cup dry white or red wine
- 2 teaspoons Dijon mustard
- ¾ cup long-grain white rice
- 2 tablespoons chopped parsley

Rinse chicken, pat dry, and set aside.

Cook bacon in a 3- to 4-quart pan over medium heat until crisp (about 5 minutes), stirring often. Lift out with a slotted spoon, drain, and set aside.

Increase heat to medium-high and add chicken to pan, skin side down. Cook, turning as needed, until well browned on all sides (about 5 minutes). Remove chicken from pan and set aside.

Add garlic, onion, and mushrooms to pan; cook, stirring occasionally, until mushrooms are soft (about 7 minutes). Add broth, wine, and mustard; bring to a boil. Stir in rice, then return chicken and bacon to pan. Reduce heat, cover, and simmer until liquid has been absorbed and chicken meat near thighbone is no longer pink; cut to test (about 25 minutes). Divide chicken and rice mixture between 2 dinner plates and sprinkle with parsley. Makes 2 servings.

Per serving: 633 calories, 26 g protein, 63 g carbohydrates, 30 g total fat, 91 mg cholesterol, 914 mg sodium

*Simple elegance is easy to achieve: just get out your best china,
set a bowl of fresh flowers on the table, and put Spinach-stuffed Game Hens
(recipe on facing page) and Brandied Cream Potato Batons (recipe on page 67)
on the menu. Scoop the savory, rosemary-scented stuffing from the hens,
then serve the golden-skinned birds whole or cut in half.*

Spinach-stuffed Game Hens

Preparation time: About 20 minutes

Roasting time: About 45 minutes

Elegant little game hens, filled with savory rice dressing and basted with garlic butter, make a perfect entrée for two. Serve Brandied Cream Potato Batons (page 67) on the side, and you have a meal worthy of a celebration.

> **Spinach-Rice Stuffing (recipe follows)**
> 2 **Rock Cornish game hens (about 1 lb. *each*), thawed if frozen**
> 3 **tablespoons butter or margarine, melted**
> 1 **clove garlic, minced or pressed**
> 1½ **tablespoons minced green onion**
> ⅛ **teaspoon liquid hot pepper seasoning**

Prepare Spinach-Rice Stuffing. Reserve hen necks and giblets for other uses; rinse hens inside and out and pat dry. Spoon half the stuffing into cavity of each hen, then truss hens with kitchen twine.

Combine butter, garlic, onion, and hot pepper seasoning. Place hens, breast down, on a rack in a small roasting pan. Brush liberally with butter mixture, reserving extra mixture for basting. Roast hens in a 425° oven for 15 minutes; baste, then carefully turn over and baste again. Continue to roast, breast up, until meat near thighbone is no longer pink; cut to test (about 30 more minutes).

Remove twine from hens. Serve whole, scooping out stuffing to eat. Or split each hen through breastbone; spoon stuffing onto a platter or 2 plates, cut through backs of hens, and set hen halves atop stuffing. Makes 2 servings.

Spinach-Rice Stuffing. Heat 2 tablespoons **olive oil** in a wide frying pan over medium-high heat. Add ¼ cup *each* thinly sliced **green onions** and diced **celery**. Cook, stirring, until onions are soft (about 2 minutes). Stir in 1 teaspoon chopped **fresh rosemary** or crumbled dry rosemary. Add 3 cups lightly packed chopped **fresh spinach** (rinsed and drained). Cook, stirring, until spinach is wilted (about 3 minutes). Remove from heat; stir in ½ cup **cooked rice.** Season to taste with **salt** and **pepper.**

Per serving: 846 calories, 59 g protein, 20 g carbohydrates, 58 g total fat, 222 mg cholesterol, 435 mg sodium

Grilled Turkey on Sesame Buns

Preparation time: About 15 minutes

Grilling time: About 3 minutes

Fire up your mini-grill for these summertime sandwiches. Lean turkey is a healthful alternative to red meats; to cut fat further, use reduced-calorie mayonnaise. For a tasty side dish, toss roasted bell pepper strips with Herb Vinaigrette (page 44).

> 2 **boneless, skinless turkey breast slices (about ⅓ lb. *total*), about ¼ inch thick**
> 2 **tablespoons olive oil**
> 1 **tablespoon lemon juice**
> 2 **sesame sandwich or hamburger buns, split**
> 2 **large butter lettuce leaves, rinsed and crisped**
> 1 **small pear-shaped tomato, sliced**
>   **Salt and pepper**
> 2 **tablespoons reduced-calorie or regular mayonnaise**
> 2 **teaspoons minced fresh marjoram or 1 teaspoon dry marjoram**
> ¼ **teaspoon grated lemon peel**

Rinse turkey and pat dry. Stir together oil and lemon juice; brush mixture evenly over both sides of turkey slices, then over cut surfaces of buns.

Place turkey on a lightly greased grill 4 to 6 inches above a solid bed of medium-hot coals. Cook, turning once, until meat is no longer pink in center; cut to test (about 3 minutes). Also set buns, cut sides down, on a cooler area of grill; cook until lightly toasted (about 2 minutes).

Place a lettuce leaf, a turkey slice, and half the tomato slices on bottom half of each bun. Season to taste with salt and pepper. Stir together mayonnaise, marjoram, and lemon peel and spoon half the mixture onto each sandwich; then cover with top halves of buns. Makes 2 servings.

Per serving: 377 calories, 22 g protein, 25 g carbohydrates, 21 g total fat, 54 mg cholesterol, 340 mg sodium

Chinese Stir-fried Turkey

Preparation time: About 20 minutes

Preparation time: About 20 minutes

Marinating time: At least 30 minutes

Cooking time: About 10 minutes

Cabbage, celery, jicama, and a subtly spiced sauce give this stir-fry its crisp texture and lively flavor. Try it over brown rice, in Asian-style bowls.

Oriental Marinade (recipe follows)
8 ounces turkey breast tenderloins, cut into ½-inch cubes
1 to 2 tablespoons salad oil
1 tablespoon minced fresh ginger
1 clove garlic, thinly sliced
½ teaspoon crushed red pepper flakes (optional)
1 cup shredded green cabbage
2 stalks celery, cut into thin slanting slices
3 green onions, cut into 1-inch lengths
4 ounces jicama, peeled and cut into matchstick pieces

Prepare marinade. Stir in turkey, cover, and refrigerate for at least 30 minutes or until next day.

Heat 1 tablespoon of the oil in a wide frying pan or wok over high heat. With a slotted spoon, lift turkey from marinade and drain well, reserving marinade. Add turkey to pan and cook, stirring, until no longer pink in center; cut to test (about 5 minutes). Remove turkey from pan and set aside.

If pan looks dry, add about 1 more tablespoon oil. When oil is hot, add ginger, garlic, and, if desired, pepper flakes; cook, stirring, until garlic is golden (about 30 seconds). Add cabbage, celery, onions, and jicama; cook, stirring, until celery is barely tender-crisp to bite (about 2 minutes). Stir marinade well and pour over vegetables. Cook, stirring, until sauce boils and thickens; then stir in turkey and heat through (about 2 minutes). Makes 2 servings.

Oriental Marinade. In a bowl, mix ½ cup **chicken broth;** 1 tablespoon *each* **cornstarch, soy sauce,** and **dry sherry;** 1 tablespoon **oyster sauce** or soy sauce; 2 teaspoons **Oriental sesame oil;** and ¼ teaspoon *each* **anise seeds** and **ground cinnamon.**

Per serving: 403 calories, 43 g protein, 17 g carbohydrates, 18 g total fat, 103 mg cholesterol, 1,031 mg sodium

Curried Turkey & Broccoli

Preparation time: About 15 minutes

Cooking time: About 15 minutes

End a hectic day on a comforting note with this simple curry. Alongside, you might present a salad of sliced papaya, avocado, and watercress sprigs.

2 cups broccoli flowerets
2 tablespoons butter or margarine
1 medium-size yellow onion, chopped
1 clove garlic, minced or pressed
1½ tablespoons curry powder
2 tablespoons all-purpose flour
1½ cups lowfat milk
⅛ teaspoon ground red pepper (cayenne)
¼ cup dry sherry
1½ cups bite-size pieces cooked turkey

Hot cooked rice
2 green onions, thinly sliced

Place broccoli on a steamer rack in a pan above 1 inch of boiling water; cover and cook just until tender-crisp to bite (about 4 minutes). Set aside.

Melt butter in a 4- to 5-quart pan over medium-high heat. Add yellow onion and garlic; cook, stirring often, until onion is soft (about 5 minutes). Add curry powder and cook, stirring, for 1 minute. Add flour and stir until bubbly (about 1 minute). Remove pan from heat and gradually stir in milk. Return to heat and cook, stirring, until sauce boils and thickens (about 2 minutes). Blend in red pepper and sherry. Reduce heat to low, add turkey and broccoli, and heat through (about 2 minutes).

Spoon rice onto 2 dinner plates and top with curry; sprinkle with green onions. Makes 2 servings.

Per serving: 504 calories, 44 g protein, 33 g carbohydrates, 19 g total fat, 118 mg cholesterol, 318 mg sodium

Healthy Condiments

Today's cook demands two things of any recipe: convenience and vibrant flavor. Numerous dishes in this book satisfy both requirements, but sometimes the need for convenience may limit you to the very simplest fare: a broiled chop, a baked chicken breast, or a piece of poached fish. The trick here is to add flavor. It may be tempting to reach for prepared sauces or relishes, but these can load your diet with unwanted fat and sodium. A better idea is to rely on a few lowfat, salt-free homemade condiments.

Based on fresh herbs, fruits, vegetables, and spices, the four choices we offer go together in under 20 minutes each. And because they can all be prepared in advance, you can make them when you have the time—a few hours ahead, early in the day, or even the night before. Serving suggestions accompany each recipe, but feel free to experiment with combinations other than those we suggest.

Pineapple-Mint Relish

In a small bowl, stir together 1 cup diced **fresh or drained canned pineapple,** ½ cup diced peeled **cucumber,** 2 tablespoons minced **fresh mint,** 1 tablespoon **cider vinegar,** and 1½ teaspoons **honey.** Serve, or cover and refrigerate for up to 4 hours.

Spoon relish over baked or grilled pork chops, chicken, or fish. Makes about 1 cup.

Per ¼ cup: 30 calories, 0.3 g protein, 8 g carbohydrates, 0.2 g total fat, 0 mg cholesterol, 2 mg sodium

Piquant Relish

In a small bowl, stir together 3 tablespoons **Dijon mustard;** 1 small **fresh jalapeño chile,** stemmed, seeded, and minced; ⅓ cup finely chopped **mild onion;** and 1 tablespoon **lemon juice.** Serve, or cover and refrigerate for up to 2 days.

Use relish on hamburgers, hot dogs, or sausages. Makes about ½ cup.

Per tablespoon: 10 calories, 0.1 g protein, 2 g carbohydrates, 0.4 g total fat, 0 mg cholesterol, 169 mg sodium

Spiced Fresh Peach Chutney

In a medium-size bowl, mix 1 medium-size firm-ripe **peach** (peeled, pitted, and diced), ½ cup **seedless grapes** (rinsed), 1 tablespoon **honey,** and 1 teaspoon **Dijon mustard.** Set aside.

In a small nonstick frying pan, combine 1½ teaspoons **salad oil;** ½ small **onion,** finely chopped; 2 tablespoons **golden raisins;** 1½ teaspoons **mustard seeds;** and ¼ teaspoon **ground allspice.** Cook over medium-high heat, stirring often, until onion is soft and raisins are puffy (about 5 minutes). Stir gently into peach mixture. Serve, or cover and refrigerate until next day.

Serve chutney with roast pork or chicken, or with broiled lamb chops. Makes about 1½ cups.

Per ¼ cup: 55 calories, 0.7 g protein, 11 g carbohydrates, 2 g total fat, 0 mg cholesterol, 26 mg sodium

Shallot-Tarragon Sauce

In a small pan, combine ⅓ cup minced **shallots,** ¼ cup *each* **balsamic vinegar** and **chicken broth,** and ½ teaspoon **dry tarragon.** Bring to a boil over medium-high heat; boil until all liquid has evaporated (about 6 minutes). Let cool, then stir in 3 tablespoons *each* **sour cream** and **plain nonfat yogurt.** Cover and refrigerate for at least 1 hour or until next day.

Use sauce as a dip for vegetables or as a spread on grilled poultry or meat sandwiches. Makes about ½ cup.

Per tablespoon: 21 calories, 0.7 g protein, 2 g carbohydrates, 1 g total fat, 2 mg cholesterol, 39 mg sodium

Fresh Seafood

Pictured on facing page

Broiled Swordfish with Tomato-Olive Confetti

Preparation time: About 15 minutes

Broiling time: About 8 minutes

Lean, meaty swordfish steaks with a lime-spiked tomato and green olive relish make a refreshing dinner for a summer evening. Warm tortillas and seasonal vegetables, such as plump ears of corn or slender green beans, are good companions to the main course.

> Tomato-Olive Confetti (recipe follows)
> 12 ounces swordfish steaks (about 1¼ inches thick)
> 1 teaspoon olive oil
> 1½ cups lightly packed watercress sprigs, rinsed and crisped

Prepare Tomato-Olive Confetti and set aside.

Rinse fish and pat dry; if necessary, cut into serving-size pieces. Place fish on oiled rack of a broiler pan; brush with oil. Broil about 4 inches below heat for 5 minutes. Then turn fish over with a wide spatula and continue to broil until just opaque but still moist in thickest part; cut to test (about 3 more minutes).

Place watercress on a platter or divide between 2 dinner plates. Using spatula, set fish atop watercress; top with Tomato-Olive Confetti. Makes 2 servings.

Tomato-Olive Confetti. In a small bowl, stir together 1 small **tomato,** seeded and chopped; ¼ cup **pimento-stuffed green olives,** sliced; 1 tablespoon drained **capers;** and 2 tablespoons *each* sliced **green onion, lime juice,** and **olive oil.**

Per serving: 382 calories, 35 g protein, 4 g carbohydrates, 25 g total fat, 66 mg cholesterol, 689 mg sodium

Protein-rich fish is an excellent choice for dinner any time. For a lean and colorful meal, savor Broiled Swordfish with Tomato-Olive Confetti (recipe on facing page) along with corn on the cob, warm corn tortillas, and a basket of your favorite fresh fruit.

Garlic-Lemon Red Snapper

Preparation time: About 10 minutes

Baking time: About 15 minutes

The essence of garlic and fresh lemon permeates these baked fillets. Top the fish with crisp toasted almonds, then serve with Seashells with Cauliflower Sauce (page 35) and a green salad for a wholesome, easy supper.

- 2 **boneless, skinless red snapper, rockfish, or halibut fillets (about 6 oz.** *each***), about ½ inch thick**
- 2 **tablespoons slivered almonds**
- 2 **tablespoons butter or margarine**
- 3 **cloves garlic, minced or pressed**
- 2 **tablespoons** *each* **lemon juice and chopped parsley**
- ¼ **teaspoon** *each* **paprika and grated lemon peel**
  Lemon wedges

Rinse fish, pat dry, and set aside.

Spread almonds in a 9-inch pie pan and bake in a 375° oven until golden (about 5 minutes), stirring several times. Remove almonds from pan and set aside.

Place butter in same pan and return to oven. When butter is melted, stir in garlic, lemon juice, parsley, paprika, and lemon peel. Add fish and turn to coat well, then bake until just opaque but still moist in thickest part; cut to test (about 10 minutes).

With a wide spatula, transfer fish to 2 dinner plates. Spoon butter mixture from baking pan over fish; sprinkle with almonds. Offer lemon wedges to squeeze over fish. Makes 2 servings.

Per serving: 334 calories, 37 g protein, 5 g carbohydrates, 18 g total fat, 94 mg cholesterol, 232 mg sodium

Lingcod in Mushroom-Tarragon Sauce

Preparation time: About 15 minutes

Cooking time: 25 to 30 minutes

Mild-flavored and low in fat, lingcod is ideally suited to baking; here, it's topped with mushrooms in a delicate, herb-infused cream sauce. If you can't find this Pacific fish in your market, you can use halibut, snapper, or bass with equally delicious results. Serve Presto Polenta (page 69) alongside for a fuss-free meal.

- 2 **tablespoons butter or margarine**
- 4 **ounces mushrooms, thinly sliced**
- 1 **tablespoon all-purpose flour**
- ¾ **cup milk**
- ¾ **teaspoon dry tarragon**
- ¼ **teaspoon ground white pepper**
- ¼ **cup dry white wine**
- 2 **tablespoons grated Parmesan cheese**
- ⅔ **pound boneless, skinless lingcod fillets (¾ to 1 inch thick)**
- 1 **tablespoon minced parsley**

Melt 1 tablespoon of the butter in a medium-size frying pan over medium-high heat. Add mushrooms and cook, stirring often, until lightly browned (about 7 minutes). Reduce heat to medium and add remaining 1 tablespoon butter; when butter is melted, stir in flour and cook, stirring, until bubbly (about 1 minute). Remove from heat and stir in milk, tarragon, and white pepper. Return to heat and cook, stirring, until sauce boils and thickens (about 2 minutes). Add wine and cheese; stir well. Remove from heat and set aside.

Rinse fish and pat dry; if necessary, cut into 2 equal-size pieces. Arrange fish in a shallow baking dish just large enough to hold it in a single layer. Pour mushroom sauce over fish. Bake in a 350° oven until fish is just opaque but still moist in thickest part; cut to test (15 to 20 minutes).

With a wide spatula, transfer fish to 2 dinner plates; spoon sauce over fish and sprinkle with parsley. Makes 2 servings.

Per serving: 361 calories, 34 g protein, 11 g carbohydrates, 18 g total fat, 127 mg cholesterol, 350 mg sodium

Pistachio-crusted Fish Fillets

Preparation time: About 15 minutes

Baking time: 8 to 12 minutes

Battered or breaded fish fillets are an old standby for speedy suppers. To give the traditional recipe a new look, try baking lean white fish in a coating of chopped pistachios and herbs. Homestyle accompaniments, such as creamed spinach and parsleyed new potatoes, are just right.

- ¼ **cup shelled salted pistachio nuts, finely chopped**
- 2 **tablespoons** *each* **fine dry bread crumbs and minced parsley**
- ¼ **teaspoon pepper**
- 1 **egg**
- ⅔ **pound boneless, skinless white-fleshed fish fillets (such as sole or orange roughy)**
- 2 **tablespoons butter or margarine**
- 2 **green onions, thinly sliced**
- 1 **tablespoon drained capers**
  Lemon wedges

On a sheet of wax paper or foil, combine pistachios, crumbs, parsley, and pepper.

In a pie pan, beat egg to blend; set aside. Rinse fish and pat dry; if necessary, cut into 2 equal-size pieces. Dip fish, a piece at a time, in egg; turn to coat. Lift out and drain briefly, then press both sides of each piece of fish into pistachio mixture to coat well. Arrange fish in a lightly greased baking dish just large enough to hold it in a single layer.

Melt butter in a small pan over medium heat. Add onions and capers and cook, stirring, just until onions are soft (about 2 minutes). Holding onions and capers back with a spoon, pour melted butter evenly over fish. Set onions and capers aside.

Bake fish in a 450° oven until just opaque but still moist in thickest part; cut to test (8 to 12 minutes). With a wide spatula, transfer fish to 2 dinner plates. Top fish with sautéed onions and capers; offer lemon wedges to squeeze over fish. Makes 2 servings.

Per serving: 381 calories, 35 g protein, 10 g carbohydrates, 23 g total fat, 157 mg cholesterol, 415 mg sodium

Grilled Snapper with Mint Relish

Preparation time: About 15 minutes

Grilling time: 8 to 12 minutes

The fresh, clean flavors of mint and cilantro blend with the tartness of lemon, the heat of jalapeños, and the sweetness of coconut in an unusual Indian-inspired relish for grilled fish. Carry out the theme with a curry-seasoned stir-fry of cauliflower, carrots, and red bell pepper.

- ¼ **cup lightly packed fresh mint leaves**
- ¼ **cup lightly packed cilantro leaves**
- 2 **tablespoons** *each* **lemon juice and water**
- 1 **small fresh jalapeño chile, stemmed and seeded**
- 1 **clove garlic**
- ¼ **teaspoon ground cumin**
- ¼ **cup sweetened shredded coconut**
- 2 **boneless, skinless red snapper or rockfish fillets (6 to 8 oz.** *each***)**

In a blender or food processor, whirl mint, cilantro, lemon juice, water, chile, garlic, and cumin until herbs are finely minced. Stir in coconut and set aside.

Rinse fish, pat dry, and place on a lightly greased grill 4 to 6 inches above a solid bed of hot coals. Cook until edges of fish begin to turn opaque; then slide a wide spatula beneath fillets and turn them over. Continue to cook until fish is opaque but still moist in thickest part; cut to test (total cooking time will be 8 to 12 minutes).

With spatula, transfer fish to 2 dinner plates; top with mint-cilantro mixture. Makes 2 servings.

Per serving: 253 calories, 41 g protein, 7 g carbohydrates, 6 g total fat, 73 mg cholesterol, 156 mg sodium

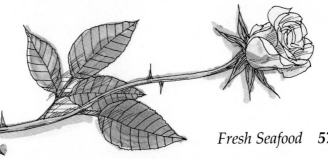

Cooking dinner is a snap when you choose Balsamic-broiled Salmon with Mint & Tabbouleh (recipe on facing page)—it gives you main course and side dish all in one. An unusual vinegar baste enhances the salmon's rich flavor; fresh mint and diced tomatoes add color to the cooling bulgur salad. To complete the meal, add glasses of chilled wine or iced tea.

Balsamic-broiled Salmon with Mint & Tabbouleh

Preparation time: About 20 minutes

Standing time: About 1 hour

Broiling time: 8 to 10 minutes

Brushed with a tart-sweet baste and strewn with cool mint, these tender salmon fillets are extra flavorful. Serve a high-fiber tabbouleh with the fish; for dessert, offer fresh strawberries topped with plain yogurt and brown sugar.

>   Mint Tabbouleh (recipe follows)
> 2 tablespoons balsamic or raspberry vinegar
> 1 tablespoon honey
> 1 teaspoon salad oil
> 2 salmon fillets (6 to 8 oz. *each*)
> ¼ cup firmly packed fresh mint leaves, minced
>   Lemon wedges and mint sprigs

Prepare Mint Tabbouleh and set aside.

In a small bowl, mix vinegar, honey, and oil. Rinse fish fillets, pat dry, and arrange slightly apart on a lightly oiled baking sheet; brush with half the vinegar mixture. Broil fish 4 to 6 inches below heat, brushing several times with remaining vinegar mixture, until just opaque but still moist in thickest part; cut to test (8 to 10 minutes).

With a wide spatula, transfer fish to 2 dinner plates; sprinkle with minced mint. Garnish with lemon wedges and mint sprigs. Serve with tabbouleh. Makes 2 servings.

Per serving without Mint Tabbouleh: 338 calories, 39 g protein, 10 g carbohydrates, 15 g total fat, 109 mg cholesterol, 90 mg sodium

Mint Tabbouleh. In a medium-size bowl, mix ¾ cup **bulgur** (cracked wheat) with 1¼ cups **boiling water;** let stand, stirring several times, until water has been absorbed (about 1 hour). Stir in 1 cup lightly packed **fresh mint leaves,** finely chopped; ¼ cup **lemon juice;** 2 tablespoons **extra-virgin olive oil** or salad oil; and 1 large **tomato,** chopped. Season to taste with **salt** and **pepper.** Serve, or cover and refrigerate for up to 1 day. Makes 2 servings.

Per serving: 327 calories, 8 g protein, 46 g carbohydrates, 15 g total fat, 0 mg cholesterol, 21 mg sodium

Poached Fish with Fennel & Tomato

Preparation time: About 15 minutes

Cooking time: About 45 minutes

The distinctly Mediterranean flavors of fresh fennel and tomatoes give this elegantly simple dish an appealing earthy quality. Serve with mixed field greens, a sliced warm baguette, and white wine.

> 1 medium-size head fennel (about 12 oz.)
> 1 tablespoon olive oil
> 1 medium-size onion, thinly sliced
> 1 can (about 14½ oz.) pear-shaped tomatoes
> ¼ teaspoon fennel seeds
> ¼ cup dry white wine
> 2 boneless, skinless mild-flavored fish fillets, such as rockfish, red snapper, or lingcod (about 6 oz. *each*)
>   Salt and pepper

Remove fennel leaves and cut off tough stems. Trim bruises from fennel, then cut head into quarters lengthwise; remove and discard core. Thinly slice fennel quarters crosswise.

Heat oil in a wide frying pan over medium-high heat; add onion and sliced fennel. Cook, stirring often, until onion is limp and golden (about 15 minutes). Cut up tomatoes; then add tomatoes and their liquid, fennel seeds, and wine to pan. Bring to a boil, then reduce heat and simmer until juices are thickened and fennel is tender to bite (about 20 minutes).

Rinse fish, pat dry, and place in tomato sauce. Cover pan and simmer until fish is just opaque but still moist in thickest part; cut to test (about 10 minutes). Lift fish from pan with a wide spatula; place on 2 dinner plates. Ladle sauce over fish; season to taste with salt and pepper. Makes 2 servings.

Per serving: 299 calories, 36 g protein, 16 g carbohydrates, 10 g total fat, 60 mg cholesterol, 576 mg sodium

Stir-fried Tuna

Preparation time: About 15 minutes

Cooking time: About 11 minutes

Meaty fresh tuna is an excellent candidate for stir-frying; pair it with fresh vegetables and pungent spices, and delicious results are assured. Serve over brown rice; sip beer or ginger ale alongside.

- 1 **teaspoon cornstarch**
- 2 **tablespoons** *each* **water, dry sherry, and soy sauce**
- 1 **tablespoon sesame seeds**
- 2 **tablespoons salad oil**
- 1 **clove garlic, minced or pressed**
- 1 **tablespoon minced fresh ginger**
- 2 **cups cauliflowerets, sliced ¼ inch thick**
- ½ **teaspoon Chinese five-spice powder; or ¼ teaspoon** *each* **ground cinnamon and ground allspice**
- ½ **cup diced red bell pepper**
- 4 **green onions, cut into 1-inch lengths**
- 8 **ounces fresh tuna (such as ahi), sliced ¼ inch thick**
- ½ **teaspoon Oriental sesame oil**
  Hot cooked brown rice

In a small bowl, stir together cornstarch, water, sherry, and soy sauce; set aside.

Toast sesame seeds in a wide frying pan or wok over medium-high heat until golden (about 4 minutes), shaking pan often. Pour out seeds and set aside. Increase heat to high and add 1 tablespoon of the salad oil to pan; when oil is hot, add garlic, ginger, and cauliflower. Cook, stirring, until cauliflower is tender-crisp to bite (about 4 minutes). Add five-spice, bell pepper, and onions; cook, stirring, just until onions are bright green (about 1 minute). With a slotted spoon, transfer mixture to a bowl and set aside.

Add remaining 1 tablespoon salad oil to pan; lay tuna slices in a single layer in pan. Cook for 30 seconds, then turn slices over and continue to cook until browned on outside but still pink in center; cut to test (about 30 more seconds). Lift tuna from pan. Pour cornstarch mixture into pan and bring to a boil, stirring. Return vegetable mixture and tuna to pan, add sesame oil, and stir gently until hot (about 1 minute). Spoon rice into 2 bowls; top with tuna mixture and sprinkle with sesame seeds. Makes 2 servings.

Per serving: 385 calories, 31 g protein, 15 g carbohydrates, 23 g total fat, 43 mg cholesterol, 1,093 mg sodium

Hot & Spicy Shrimp

Preparation time: About 15 minutes

Cooking time: About 19 minutes

East meets West in this seafood stir-fry, a harmonious blend of mushrooms, onion, tomato, and shrimp seasoned with fiery chili paste. Ladle it into bowls over chunks of crusty bread.

- 2 **tablespoons butter or margarine**
- 1 **medium-size yellow onion, chopped**
- 2 **cloves garlic, minced or pressed**
- 1 **large tomato, peeled, seeded, and chopped**
- ½ **to 1 teaspoon (or to taste) hot Chinese chili paste with garlic (or other hot chili paste)**
- 4 **ounces mushrooms, thinly sliced**
- ½ **cup dry white wine**
- 8 **ounces large raw shrimp, shelled, deveined, and halved lengthwise**
- ½ **cup chicken broth**
- 1 **tablespoon chopped parsley**
- 1 **green onion, thinly sliced**

Melt butter in a wide frying pan or wok over medium-high heat. Add yellow onion and garlic and cook, stirring often, until onion is soft (about 7 minutes). Stir in tomato, chili paste, mushrooms, and wine. Bring to a boil over high heat; boil until almost all wine has evaporated (about 8 minutes).

Reduce heat to medium; add shrimp and cook, stirring often, just until shrimp begin to curl (about 2 minutes). Stir in broth, parsley, and green onion. Continue to cook until shrimp are just opaque in center; cut to test (about 2 more minutes). Ladle into 2 bowls. Makes 2 servings.

Per serving: 266 calories, 22 g protein, 12 g carbohydrates, 15 g total fat, 171 mg cholesterol, 514 mg sodium

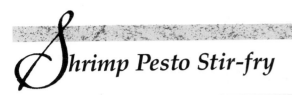

Shrimp Pesto Stir-fry

Preparation time: About 15 minutes

Cooking time: About 10 minutes

Emerald pesto, pink shrimp, and multicolored vegetables team up for an attractive one-pan supper. To complete the meal, offer chewy cooked barley.

   Quick Pesto (recipe follows) or 2 tablespoons Classic Pesto (page 32)
2 **tablespoons butter or margarine**
1 **carrot, thinly sliced**
1 **small onion, cut into 1-inch squares**
1 **small zucchini, thinly sliced**
8 **small mushrooms, thinly sliced**
½ *each* **small green and red bell pepper, seeded and thinly sliced**
12 **ounces medium-size raw shrimp, shelled and deveined**
   Basil sprigs (optional)
   Grated Parmesan cheese (optional)

Prepare Quick Pesto; set aside.

Melt 1 tablespoon of the butter in a wide frying pan or wok over medium-high heat. Add carrot and onion and stir for 2 minutes. Add zucchini, mushrooms, and red and green bell pepper; stir until carrot is tender-crisp to bite (about 2 minutes). Remove vegetables from pan; keep warm.

Melt remaining 1 tablespoon butter in pan, then stir in pesto. Add shrimp and cook, stirring, until just opaque in center; cut to test (about 4 minutes). Return vegetables to pan and stir until hot and coated with sauce (about 2 minutes).

Spoon shrimp mixture onto 2 dinner plates; garnish with basil sprigs and sprinkle with cheese, if desired. Makes 2 servings.

Quick Pesto. Mix 1 tablespoon grated **Parmesan cheese,** 2 teaspoons *each* **dry basil** and minced **parsley,** and 1 tablespoon **olive oil** or salad oil.

Per serving: 365 calories, 31 g protein, 12 g carbohydrates, 22 g total fat, 242 mg cholesterol, 385 mg sodium

Lime & Chipotle Scallops

Preparation time: About 10 minutes

Cooking time: About 8 minutes

Chilling time: At least 1½ hours

Canned chipotle chiles, sold in Mexican markets and some supermarkets, add a smoky, subtly hot accent to a cold entrée that's reminiscent of classic seviche. You might flank each serving with a salsa-topped avocado half and a mound of corn chips.

8 **ounces sea or bay scallops**
2 **teaspoons salad oil**
¼ **cup minced shallots**
¼ **teaspoon minced canned chipotle chiles in sauce; or ¼ teaspoon crushed red pepper flakes**
¼ **cup** *each* **lime juice, distilled white vinegar, and water**
4 **ounces jicama**
2 **tablespoons minced cilantro**
   Lime wedges

Rinse and drain scallops. If scallops are large, cut them into quarters. Set aside.

Heat oil in a medium-size frying pan over medium heat. Add shallots and chiles; cook, stirring, until shallots are soft (about 3 minutes). Stir in lime juice, vinegar, and water; bring to a boil over high heat. Add scallops, reduce heat, cover, and simmer until scallops are just opaque in center; cut to test (about 2 minutes).

With a slotted spoon, transfer scallops to a bowl. Boil pan juices over high heat until reduced by half (about 3 minutes), then pour over scallops. Cover and refrigerate until cool (at least 1½ hours) or for up to 8 hours.

Just before serving, peel jicama and cut into ¼-inch-thick matchstick pieces. Gently mix jicama with scallops and spoon into 2 shallow bowls; distribute liquid evenly between bowls. Garnish with cilantro and lime wedges. Makes 2 servings.

Per serving: 187 calories, 20 g protein, 14 g carbohydrates, 6 g total fat, 37 mg cholesterol, 203 mg sodium

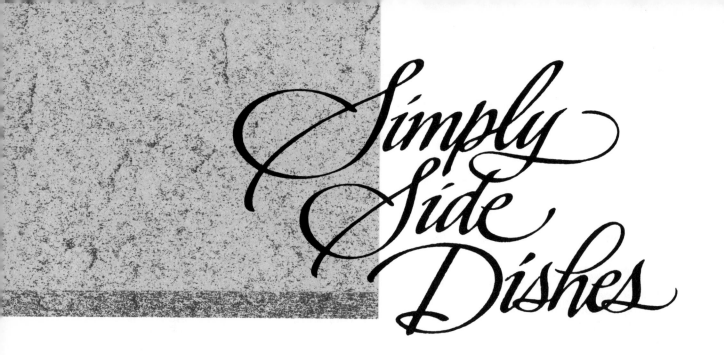

Simply Side Dishes

Pictured on facing page

Baby Squash Stew

Preparation time: About 20 minutes

Cooking time: About 22 minutes

Pearl onions and miniature summer squash in an herb-scented cream sauce are a show-stopping accompaniment for lamb chops or beef steaks. Use just one kind of squash, or combine several varieties for an especially attractive dish. You'll find these tiny jewels in the specialty produce section of your supermarket.

8	ounces baby squash, such as pattypan (*each* about 1½ inches in diameter), crookneck or straightneck (*each* about 3 inches long), or yellow or green zucchini (*each* about 3 inches long)
1	cup small pearl onions (*each* about ½ inch in diameter)
1¼	cups chicken broth
⅓	cup dry vermouth or white wine
1	clove garlic, minced or pressed
½	teaspoon dry thyme
1	bay leaf
⅛	teaspoon *each* dry basil and dry oregano
½	cup whipping cream

Trim off and discard stems from squash, then set squash aside. Place onions in a bowl, pour in enough boiling water to cover, and let stand for 5 minutes. Drain; let cool briefly. Cut off root ends, then slip off skins. Set onions aside.

In a 2- to 3-quart pan, combine broth, vermouth, garlic, thyme, bay leaf, basil, and oregano. Bring to a boil over high heat; add onions. Reduce heat, cover, and simmer until onions are tender-crisp when pierced (about 10 minutes). Add squash; bring to a boil over high heat, then reduce heat and simmer until squash and onions are tender when pierced (about 5 minutes). With a slotted spoon, lift vegetables from pan and set aside. Remove and discard bay leaf.

Add cream to cooking broth, bring to a rapid boil over high heat, and boil, stirring often, until sauce is reduced to about ½ cup (about 7 minutes). Add vegetables to sauce and stir until hot. To serve, divide between 2 small bowls. Makes 2 servings.

Per serving: 271 calories, 5 g protein, 21 g carbohydrates, 20 g total fat, 66 mg cholesterol, 652 mg sodium

Tiny, tender, jewel-bright miniature squash star in our Baby Squash Stew
(recipe on facing page). Yellow and green pattypans, petite zucchini, and pearl
onions poached in a delicate cream sauce make a knockout accompaniment
to thyme-garnished broiled lamb chops. Warm bakery rolls and rich red
wine round out this attractive dinner.

Mediterranean Spinach

Preparation time: About 15 minutes

Cooking time: About 6 minutes

It's easy to make ordinary spinach extraordinary: just team it with salty feta cheese, ripe olives, and chopped tomatoes. This colorful dish is perfect with broiled lamb chops or hamburgers.

- 2 teaspoons olive oil
- 1 clove garlic, minced or pressed
- ¼ cup thinly sliced green onions
- ¼ teaspoon dry dill weed
- 2 small firm-ripe pear-shaped tomatoes, chopped
- 1 pound spinach, stemmed, rinsed, and drained
- ¼ cup crumbled feta cheese
- 1 small can (about 3¼ oz.) ripe olives, drained

In a 3- to 4-quart pan, combine oil, garlic, onions, and dill weed. Cook over medium-high heat, stirring often, until onions are soft (about 2 minutes); then add tomatoes and cook, stirring, for 1 minute. With a slotted spoon, transfer mixture to a bowl and set aside.

Add spinach to pan and stir over medium heat just until wilted (about 3 minutes). With a slotted spoon, transfer to a serving plate and spread out slightly. Top with onion-tomato mixture and sprinkle with cheese and olives. Makes 2 servings.

Per serving: 197 calories, 9 g protein, 15 g carbohydrates, 14 g total fat, 15 mg cholesterol, 728 mg sodium

Simply Perfect Eggplant

Preparation time: About 15 minutes

Cooking time: About 10 minutes

It's quite a claim, but we think you'll agree: this eggplant dish really is perfect. Cut into "coins," oven-roasted, and topped with sautéed vegetables, slender Oriental eggplant makes a sublime partner for grilled chicken. Add a loaf of crusty bread, and you have the ideal menu for a summer celebration.

- About 3 tablespoons olive oil
- 3 medium-size Oriental eggplants, cut crosswise into ½-inch-thick slices
- 2 tablespoons drained, finely chopped dried tomatoes packed in oil
- 1 small onion, finely chopped
- 4 ounces mushrooms, minced
- 1 small red bell pepper, seeded and chopped
- 1 tablespoon chopped parsley
- 1 teaspoon *each* chopped fresh oregano and fresh marjoram; or ½ teaspoon *each* dry oregano and dry marjoram
- Salt and pepper

Coat a 10- by 15-inch baking pan with a little of the oil. Lay eggplant slices in a single layer in pan; brush with about 2 tablespoons of the oil. Bake in a 425° oven until browned and very soft when pressed (about 10 minutes).

Meanwhile, heat remaining oil (about 1 tablespoon) in a medium-size frying pan over medium heat. Add tomatoes, onion, mushrooms, bell pepper, parsley, oregano, and marjoram. Cook, stirring often, until vegetables are soft and mushrooms are lightly browned (about 10 minutes).

Arrange eggplant slices on a serving plate and top with vegetable mixture. Season to taste with salt and pepper. Makes 2 servings.

Per serving: 297 calories, 4 g protein, 17 g carbohydrates, 25 g total fat, 0 mg cholesterol, 334 mg sodium

Green Bean Ragout

Preparation time: About 15 minutes

Cooking time: About 20 minutes

If you're looking for an unusual presentation for green vegetables, try this vibrant tomato and green bean sauté. It's an excellent side dish for roasted turkey or other poultry.

- 8 ounces green beans, ends removed, cut into 2-inch lengths
- 1 tablespoon butter or margarine
- 1 clove garlic, minced or pressed
- 1 small onion, chopped
- 1 stalk celery, thinly sliced
- 1 large ripe tomato, peeled, seeded, and chopped
- 1 tablespoon chopped fresh basil or 1½ teaspoons dry basil

  Salt and pepper

In a wide frying pan, bring 1 inch of water to a boil over high heat. Add beans and cook until barely tender when pierced (about 7 minutes). Drain, rinse with cold water, and set aside.

Return pan to medium heat and add butter. When butter is melted, stir in garlic, onion, and celery. Cook, stirring occasionally, until vegetables just begin to brown (about 10 minutes). Add tomato, basil, and beans; cook, stirring gently, just until beans are heated through (about 3 minutes). Season to taste with salt and pepper. Makes 2 servings.

Per serving: 111 calories, 3 g protein, 14 g carbohydrates, 6 g total fat, 16 mg cholesterol, 89 mg sodium

Barley & Lentils with Mint

Preparation time: About 10 minutes

Cooking time: About 40 minutes

Double your dose of carbohydrates and fiber by combining grains and legumes in a sturdy pilaf. Serve the savory blend with chicken or pork, or with a vegetable curry for a meatless meal.

- ⅓ cup lentils
- ⅓ cup pearl barley
- 2 cups chicken broth
- 1 tablespoon butter or margarine
- ¼ cup sliced almonds
- 2 tablespoons golden raisins
- ¼ cup minced fresh mint

  Plain lowfat yogurt (optional)

Sort lentils and remove any debris; then rinse and drain lentils and barley. In a 1½- to 2-quart pan, bring broth to a boil over high heat. Add lentils and barley, reduce heat, cover, and simmer until barley is tender to bite and liquid has been absorbed (about 40 minutes).

Meanwhile, melt butter in a medium-size frying pan over medium heat. Add almonds and raisins; cook, stirring, until almonds are golden and raisins are puffy (about 3 minutes). Set aside.

To serve, stir almonds and raisins into lentil-barley mixture, spoon onto 2 plates, and sprinkle with mint. Offer yogurt to add to taste, if desired. Makes 2 servings.

Per serving: 401 calories, 18 g protein, 54 g carbohydrates, 14 g total fat, 16 mg cholesterol, 1,054 mg sodium

*Are you craving comfort food tonight? Pamper yourselves
with this homey, satisfying meal—fluffy Garlic Mashed Potatoes (recipe
on facing page), Veal Patties with Marsala Sauce (recipe on page 43), steamed
baby carrots topped with aromatic rosemary sprigs, and
mugs of cold, foamy beer.*

Pictured on facing page

Garlic Mashed Potatoes

Preparation time: About 10 minutes

Cooking time: About 25 minutes

Nothing beats the creamy goodness of homemade mashed potatoes—and they're even better when subtly accented with roasted garlic and fresh rosemary. Whip up a batch to offer alongside Veal Patties with Marsala Sauce (page 43).

2	medium-size russet potatoes, scrubbed and quartered
6	cloves garlic, unpeeled
1	teaspoon olive oil
2	tablespoons butter or margarine
⅓	cup lowfat milk
1	teaspoon chopped fresh rosemary (optional)
	Salt and pepper

Place potatoes in a 2- to 3-quart pan and add enough water to cover by 1 inch. Cover pan and bring to boil over high heat; reduce heat to medium-high and boil gently until potatoes are soft when pierced (about 20 minutes). Drain. Let potatoes cool slightly, then remove and discard peel. Put potatoes through a ricer or mash well with a fork or potato masher.

While potatoes are cooking, place garlic on a 5- by 5-inch piece of foil. Drizzle oil over garlic, then wrap foil around garlic to enclose. Bake in a 350° oven until garlic cloves are soft when pressed (about 20 minutes). Remove garlic from foil and let cool slightly.

Melt butter in milk in a 2- to 3-quart pan over medium-high heat. When mixture is bubbly, squeeze soft garlic from each clove into pan. Beat well with a whisk to blend; then add potatoes and continue to whisk until smooth and thick (total beating time will be about 5 minutes). Remove from heat and stir in rosemary, if desired. Season to taste with salt and pepper. Makes 2 servings.

Per serving: 281 calories, 5 g protein, 33 g carbohydrates, 15 g total fat, 34 mg cholesterol, 151 mg sodium

Pictured on page 50

Brandied Cream Potato Batons

Preparation time: About 15 minutes

Cooking time: About 30 minutes

To turn the humble potato into an elegant accompaniment, sauté slender strips in butter until golden, then coat them with a rich brandy and cream sauce. Serve alongside an equally opulent main course, such as filet mignon or game hens.

1	tablespoon butter or margarine
12	ounces white thin-skinned potatoes, scrubbed and cut into ¼-inch-thick sticks
¼	cup brandy
½	cup chicken broth
½	cup whipping cream
	Freshly ground pepper
	Freshly grated nutmeg
	Parsley sprigs

Melt butter in a medium-size frying pan over medium-high heat. Add potatoes. Cook, occasionally turning potatoes gently with a wide spatula, just until potatoes begin to turn pale gold (about 10 minutes).

Add brandy and broth; reduce heat, cover, and simmer until potatoes are tender when pierced (about 15 minutes). Add cream. Continue to simmer, gently turning potatoes with spatula, until cream has been absorbed (about 5 minutes).

Spoon potatoes into a warm serving dish (or divide between 2 plates). Sprinkle potatoes generously with pepper and nutmeg; garnish with parsley. Makes 2 servings.

Per serving: 394 calories, 6 g protein, 39 g carbohydrates, 25 g total fat, 82 mg cholesterol, 337 mg sodium

each Pilaf

Preparation time: About 15 minutes

Cooking time: About 29 minutes

There's almost no limit to the ways you can serve rice. Here, the versatile grain stars in a hearty pilaf studded with fresh peach chunks, mushrooms, and crisp cashews. You might try this healthful, high-fiber offering alongside roasted poultry or lamb.

- 1 **tablespoon butter or margarine**
- 4 **ounces mushrooms, thinly sliced**
- ½ **cup long-grain white rice**
- 1¼ **cups chicken broth**
- 1 **medium-size firm-ripe peach**
  About 1 tablespoon lemon juice
- 2 **green onions, thinly sliced**
- 2 **tablespoons salted roasted cashews**

Melt butter in a 1½- to 2-quart pan over medium-high heat. Add mushrooms and cook, stirring occasionally, until lightly browned (about 7 minutes).

Add rice and cook, stirring, until opaque (about 2 minutes). Add broth; bring to a boil, reduce heat, cover, and simmer until rice is tender to bite (about 20 minutes).

Meanwhile, peel and pit peach, then cut into ½-inch chunks and mix with lemon juice to coat well. When rice is done, gently stir in peach, onions, and cashews. Makes 2 servings.

Per serving: 331 calories, 8 g protein, 51 g carbohydrates, 11 g total fat, 16 mg cholesterol, 733 mg sodium

roccoli with Pine Nuts & Rice

Preparation time: About 10 minutes

Cooking time: About 41 minutes

This chili-accented combination of simmered brown rice and broccoli is so substantial, you need add only a simply cooked steak, chop, or fish fillet to make a complete meal.

- 3 **tablespoons pine nuts or slivered almonds**
- 2 **teaspoons olive oil or salad oil**
- ⅓ **cup long-grain brown rice**
- ¼ **cup golden raisins**
- ½ **teaspoon chili powder**
- 1½ **cups chicken broth**
- 8 **ounces broccoli**

Toast pine nuts in a medium-size frying pan over medium heat until golden (about 4 minutes), stirring often. Pour out of pan and set aside.

Increase heat to medium-high. To pan, add oil, rice, raisins, and chili powder. Cook, stirring, until rice is opaque (about 2 minutes). Add broth, stir well, and bring to a boil; then reduce heat, cover, and simmer until rice is barely tender to bite (about 25 minutes).

Meanwhile, cut flowerets off broccoli and set aside. Cut off and discard tough ends of stalks; thinly slice tender sections of stalks.

After rice has cooked for 25 minutes, lay broccoli flowerets and sliced stalks atop rice. Cover and continue to cook until broccoli is just tender to bite (about 10 more minutes). Gently stir broccoli into rice; sprinkle with pine nuts. Makes 2 servings.

Per serving: 331 calories, 12 g protein, 47 g carbohydrates, 14 g total fat, 0 mg cholesterol, 782 mg sodium

Microwaved Grains

When you need to get dinner on the table in minimal time, the microwave is an ideal assistant. It's especially helpful in preparing simple side dishes; while the main course cooks on your range, you can zap one of the following grain specialties in your microwave to complete the meal.

Certain grains are particularly good choices for microwaving. Polenta (coarsely ground Italian cornmeal) turns out extra creamy and smooth, and you avoid the constant stirring required by the traditional recipe. Embellish your polenta with butter and Parmesan cheese; or serve it as you would pasta, topped with your favorite meat or tomato sauce.

Microwaved couscous is fluffier and more tender than the stovetop-simmered grain; onion and red bell pepper jazz up our version. Bulgur pilaf, superb with barbecued lamb, beef, or chicken, offers a delicious change of pace from rice.

In microwaving grains, standing time is the key to success. Use those extra minutes to set the table, put the finishing touches on your entrée, or just relax with a glass of wine.

Presto Polenta

In a 1-quart microwave-safe bowl, combine ½ cup **polenta** or yellow cornmeal and 1 tablespoon **butter** or margarine. Stir in 1 cup *each* **chicken broth** and **water.** Cover and microwave on **HIGH (100%)** for 8 minutes, stirring after 5 minutes. Let stand, covered, for about 5 minutes or until polenta is soft and creamy and all liquid has been absorbed. Dot with 1 tablespoon **butter** or margarine and stir until melted; then sprinkle with grated **Parmesan cheese.** Season to taste with **salt** and **pepper.** Makes 2 servings.

Per serving: 241 calories, 5 g protein, 27 g carbohydrates, 13 g total fat, 31 mg cholesterol, 611 mg sodium

Quickest Couscous

Place 1 tablespoon **butter** or margarine in a 1-quart microwave-safe casserole. Microwave, uncovered, on **HIGH (100%)** for 1 minute or until melted. Stir in ½ small **onion,** finely chopped, and ½ small **red bell pepper,** seeded and finely chopped; cover and microwave on **HIGH (100%)** for 5 minutes. Stir in ½ cup **couscous** and 1 cup **chicken broth;** cover and microwave on **HIGH (100%)** for 2 minutes or until boiling. Let stand, covered, for about 3 minutes or until couscous is tender to bite. Makes 2 servings.

Per serving: 244 calories, 8 g protein, 38 g carbohydrates, 7 g total fat, 16 mg cholesterol, 557 mg sodium

Speedy Cracked Wheat Pilaf

Place 1 tablespoon **butter** or margarine in a 1-quart microwave-safe casserole. Microwave, uncovered, on **HIGH (100%)** for 1 minute or until melted. Add ½ cup **bulgur** (cracked wheat) and stir to coat thoroughly with butter; then stir in 1¼ cups **chicken broth.** Cover and microwave on **HIGH (100%)** for 10 minutes, stirring after 5 minutes. Stir in 2 tablespoons thinly sliced **green onion** and ¼ cup thawed **frozen peas;** cover and let stand for about 10 minutes or until bulgur is tender to bite and all liquid has been absorbed. Fluff pilaf with a fork, then serve. Makes 2 servings.

Per serving: 203 calories, 7 g protein, 30 g carbohydrates, 7 g total fat, 16 mg cholesterol, 702 mg sodium

Sweet Endings

Pictured on facing page

Individual Pavlovas with a Fruit Rainbow

Preparation time: About 40 minutes

Baking time: About 55 minutes

Resting on a pink foam of whipped cream and puréed berries, individual free-form meringues are topped with a kiwi and passion fruit sauce and flanked with golden papaya slices and still more berries. This elegant dessert is the perfect conclusion to a meal of Pistachio-crusted Fish Fillets (page 57) and Green Bean Ragout (page 65).

> **Individual Meringues (recipe follows)**
> **Berry Cream (recipe follows)**
> **Kiwi–Passion Fruit Sauce (recipe follows)**

½ **medium-size papaya, peeled, seeded, and thinly sliced crosswise**

⅓ **cup raspberries or hulled, thinly sliced strawberries**

Prepare Individual Meringues. While meringues are baking, prepare Berry Cream and Kiwi–Passion Fruit Sauce.

To assemble desserts, spread half the Berry Cream on each of 2 dessert plates. Place a meringue off-center atop cream on each plate; arrange papaya and raspberries beside meringues. Offer Kiwi–Passion Fruit Sauce to ladle over each serving. Makes 2 servings.

Individual Meringues. In a medium-size bowl, beat 2 **egg whites** with an electric mixer on high speed until foamy. Gradually add ¼ cup **sugar,** beating until meringue holds stiff peaks. Beat in ¼ teaspoon **vinegar** and 1 teaspoon **cornstarch.** Spoon meringue onto a greased baking sheet in 2 equal-size mounds, spacing evenly. Bake in a 250° oven until meringues are pale golden and feel firm when gently pressed (about 55 minutes). Let cool completely on baking sheet on a rack. To remove meringues from baking sheet, slide a wide spatula beneath them to loosen; then lift off.

Berry Cream. In a blender or food processor, whirl ½ cup **raspberries** or hulled, halved strawberries with 2 teaspoons **sugar** until smoothly puréed. In a bowl, beat ⅓ cup **whipping cream** until it holds stiff peaks. Fold in berry purée. Cover and refrigerate until ready to use.

Kiwi–Passion Fruit Sauce. Peel and quarter 1 large **kiwi fruit;** whirl in a blender or food processor until smoothly puréed. Halve 1 ripe **passion fruit;** scoop pulp and seeds into blender (or omit passion fruit and use 1 more kiwi fruit). Whirl just until blended. Cover and refrigerate sauce until ready to use.

Per serving: 340 calories, 6 g protein, 54 g carbohydrates, 13 g total fat, 44 mg cholesterol, 76 mg sodium

Show-stopping? Yes. Hard to make? Not at all. Individual Pavlovas with a Fruit Rainbow (recipe on facing page) go together surprisingly easily. Chewy baked meringues and fresh fruit are arranged on a pastel-pink raspberry cream purée; a simple sauce of kiwi and passion fruit is spooned over all. Accompany this fabulous springtime dessert with espresso in dainty demitasse cups.

71

Frozen Berry Yogurt

Preparation time: About 10 minutes

Freezing time: 15 to 30 minutes (plus additional standing time for firmer texture, if desired)

With the help of modern kitchen tools, making homemade frozen desserts is easier than ever. The cylinder ice cream freezer frees you from bothering with rock salt and ice; you just use the cylinders cold from your freezer. This creamy fruit-and-yogurt dessert can be concocted in minutes; it's a smooth finish to any light meal.

- ⅔ **cup fresh or thawed frozen raspberries, boysenberries, or blackberries**
- 5 **to 7 tablespoons sugar**
- 1 **teaspoon vanilla**
- 1⅓ **cups plain regular or lowfat yogurt**

In a blender or food processor, combine berries, sugar, vanilla, and yogurt; whirl until mixture is smooth and sugar is dissolved. If desired, press mixture through a fine sieve to remove seeds; discard seeds.

Pour mixture into frozen container of a cylinder ice cream freezer and freeze according to manufacturer's directions until desired consistency is achieved. For soft-frozen yogurt, freeze for 15 to 30 minutes; remove lid and blade, then serve. For firmer texture, remove blade; then replace lid and let stand in outer case for 20 to 30 more minutes. Makes 2 servings (1 cup *each*).

Per serving: 264 calories, 6 g protein, 50 g carbohydrates, 5 g total fat, 20 mg cholesterol, 70 mg sodium

Peaches & Pralines

Preparation time: About 20 minutes

Cooking time: About 20 minutes

Cooling time: At least 10 minutes

Caramelized sugar plays a double role in this dessert. First, it's the base for a rum-cream sauce you spoon over sliced fresh peaches or nectarines; second, it turns pecan halves into crackly pralines to scatter atop the fruit. (If you have extra pralines, store them airtight for up to 1 week.) Try this Southern-style treat after a meal of fried chicken and grits.

- **Pecan Pralines (recipe follows)**
- ¼ **cup sugar**
- 2 **tablespoons whipping cream**
- 1 **tablespoon rum or brandy**
- 2 **medium-size peaches (peeled, if desired) or nectarines, pitted and sliced**

Prepare Pecan Pralines and set aside.

To caramelize sugar, place it in a heavy-bottomed 1- to 1½-quart pan over medium-high heat. Warm sugar until it melts and turns a light caramel color (about 5 minutes), shaking pan frequently to mix dry sugar with liquid as sugar melts. Watch carefully to avoid burning. When sugar is caramelized, add cream and stir until sauce is smooth (mixture will boil vigorously). Remove from heat and stir in rum. Let cool for at least 10 minutes.

Divide peaches between 2 dessert plates. Pour sauce over fruit; then top with Pecan Pralines. Makes 2 servings.

Per serving without Pecan Pralines: 212 calories, 1 g protein, 40 g carbohydrates, 5 g total fat, 17 mg cholesterol, 5 mg sodium

Pecan Pralines. In an 8- to 10-inch frying pan, combine 1 tablespoon **butter** or margarine and ¾ cup **pecan halves.** Stir over medium heat until nuts darken slightly (about 10 minutes). Drain on paper towels.

Wipe pan clean; add 6 tablespoons **sugar** and caramelize as directed at left. At once, stir in pecans and 1½ teaspoons **butter** or margarine. Immediately pour mixture onto a sheet of greased foil, pushing pecans apart with a spoon. Let cool, then break pecans apart. Makes 2 servings.

Per serving: 401 calories, 2 g protein, 42 g carbohydrates, 27 g total fat, 23 mg cholesterol, 88 mg sodium

Grapefruit & Cream

Preparation time: About 15 minutes

Cooking time: About 7 minutes

Citrus fruit offers the ideal way to jazz up winter desserts. Here, sparkling grapefruit sections and candied peel tumble over ice cream or frozen yogurt for a tempting contrast of tart and sweet flavors. The simple sundaes make a lively follow-up to a rich main course, such as Lingcod in Mushroom-Tarragon Sauce (page 56).

- 1 **medium-size pink grapefruit**
- 2 **tablespoons orange-flavored liqueur**
  About 1 cup water
- 2 **teaspoons *each* honey and sugar**
  About 1 pint vanilla ice cream or frozen yogurt

With a vegetable peeler, pare peel (colored part only) from half of grapefruit. Cut peel crosswise into very thin slivers; set aside.

With a sharp knife, cut remaining peel and all white membrane from outside of grapefruit.

Holding fruit over a bowl to catch juice, cut between membrane to free segments; place segments in bowl. Squeeze juice from membrane into bowl, then discard membrane. Drain juice from bowl and reserve. Stir 1 tablespoon of the liqueur into grapefruit segments. Set aside.

In a 1- to 1½-quart pan, combine slivered peel and ½ cup of the water. Bring to a boil over high heat; boil for 2 minutes, then drain. Repeat, using ½ cup more water.

Measure reserved juice; if necessary, add enough water to make ¼ cup. To drained peel in pan, add juice, honey, and sugar. Bring to a boil over high heat; boil, stirring occasionally, until peel is translucent and syrup is reduced to 2 table-spoons (about 3 minutes). Remove from heat and stir in remaining 1 tablespoon liqueur.

Place a scoop of ice cream in each of 2 dessert bowls. Spoon grapefruit segments over ice cream; top with peel and syrup. Makes 2 servings.

Per serving: 394 calories, 6 g protein, 58 g carbohydrates, 14 g total fat, 60 mg cholesterol, 116 mg sodium

Broiled Bananas & Pineapple

Preparation time: About 15 minutes

Broiling time: About 6 minutes

This hot fruit dessert is an excellent choice all year round, especially when other fresh fruit is scarce. Try it as a tasty ending to a winter meal such as Lamb Shanks with Hominy & Mint Aïoli (page 45)—or enjoy it for breakfast. Cool sour cream is a favorite topping, but choose leaner yogurt if you prefer.

- 1 **large ripe banana**
- 4 **slices fresh or drained canned pineapple**
- 2 **tablespoons firmly packed brown sugar**
- 1 **tablespoon butter or margarine**
  Sour cream or plain lowfat yogurt

Peel banana; cut in half crosswise, then cut each half in half lengthwise.

Arrange banana pieces and pineapple slices in a single layer in a 9- or 10-inch pie pan. Sprinkle with sugar and dot with butter. Broil about 6 inches below heat until fruit is glazed (about 6 minutes), basting a few times. Spoon hot fruit into 2 dessert dishes and top each serving with sour cream; pour any remaining hot butter sauce from pan over sour cream. Makes 2 servings.

Per serving: 244 calories, 1 g protein, 49 g carbohydrates, 7 g total fat, 16 mg cholesterol, 65 mg sodium

End a spicy meal on a light note with Fresh Fruit in Lemon-Ginger
Syrup (recipe on facing page). Sweet seedless grapes and melon cubes in a
cool, minted syrup refresh the palate; tongue-tingling champagne is
ideal for sipping alongside.

Fresh Fruit in Lemon-Ginger Syrup

Preparation time: About 15 minutes

Cooking time: About 7 minutes

Cooling time: About 1 hour

For a light, refreshing finale to a spicy meal or Oriental supper, offer your choice of seasonal fruit in a gingery fresh lemon syrup.

> 1 **small lemon**
> 1 **piece fresh ginger (about 1 by 2 inches)**
> ¼ **cup sugar**
> ¾ **cup water**
> 2 **tablespoons lightly packed fresh mint leaves**
> 2 **cups fresh fruit, such as seedless grapes; cantaloupe, honeydew melon, or papaya chunks; or hulled, halved strawberries (or use a combination)**
>   **Mint sprigs**

With a vegetable peeler, pare 4 strips of peel (colored part only) from lemon. Cut 2 strips crosswise into very thin slivers; place slivers and remaining 2 strips in a 1½- to 2-quart pan.

Mince half the ginger; thinly slice remainder. Add all ginger to pan along with sugar, water, and mint leaves. Bring to a boil over high heat, stirring often. Reduce heat and boil gently until reduced by half (about 7 minutes). Remove from heat. With a slotted spoon, remove and discard lemon strips, ginger slices, and mint leaves.

Let syrup cool for about 1 hour. Divide fruit between 2 dessert bowls or glasses; spoon syrup equally over fruit. Garnish with mint sprigs. Makes 2 servings.

Per serving: 153 calories, 0.9 g protein, 39 g carbohydrates, 0.5 g total fat, 0 mg cholesterol, 3 mg sodium

Figs with Orange Liqueur & Mascarpone

Preparation time: About 10 minutes

Cooking time (for pine nuts): About 4 minutes

At their flavorful peak in late summer, plump ripe figs pair up with rich Italian cream cheese and toasted pine nuts in this sophisticated ending for a warm-weather meal (such as Broiled Swordfish with Tomato-Olive Confetti, page 54). Mascarpone is sold in specialty cheese shops and many Italian delicatessens; if you can't find it, substitute a first-rate cream cheese.

> 1 **tablespoon pine nuts**
> 4 **medium-size ripe figs**
> 1 **tablespoon orange-flavored liqueur or 2 teaspoons thawed frozen orange juice concentrate**
> ⅓ **to ½ cup mascarpone cheese or best-quality soft cream cheese**
>   **Mint sprigs (optional)**

Toast pine nuts in a small frying pan over medium heat until golden (about 4 minutes), stirring often. Let cool.

Trim stems from figs, if desired; then cut each fig in half lengthwise. Arrange 4 halves on each of 2 dessert plates. Drizzle figs with liqueur (or brush lightly with orange juice concentrate).

In center of each plate, mound half the mascarpone, shaping it into a cone with a small spatula. Sprinkle cheese with pine nuts; garnish each plate with mint sprigs, if desired. To eat, spread cheese and pine nuts on figs; eat with a fork or pick up with your fingers. Makes 2 servings.

Per serving: 268 calories, 5 g protein, 23 g carbohydrates, 18 g total fat, 47 mg cholesterol, 129 mg sodium

Sauces & Syrups

With a few all-purpose sauces on hand, you'll find it easy to add a lively flourish to many dishes. Savory choices such as chutneys may be high on your list of essential embellishments—but don't forget the value of sweet selections. Fruit, spice, sugar, and chocolate can be transformed into an array of toppings that make desserts, snacks, and breakfast specialties sparkle. When your sweet tooth nudges you into a little splurge, treat yourself to the syrups and sauces on this page.

For delicious decadence, top ice cream, brownies, pound cake, and berries with our irresistible fudge sauce; or just indulge and eat it by the spoonful! Spoon bright and sunny berry sauces over vanilla pudding, all kinds of ice cream, baked meringues, fresh fruit, or even dense chocolate cake.

A trio of syrups offers a range of sweet possibilities. Both Cherry-Maple Syrup and Spiced Apple Syrup add a homemade touch to pancakes and waffles; they're also delightful drizzled over sugar-sprinkled crêpes, hot biscuits, or poached apples or pears. And Spiced Rum Syrup instantly turns plain sliced fruit, such as oranges, melon, or bananas, into a sophisticated dessert.

Fudge Sauce

In a 1-quart pan, combine ⅓ cup **whipping cream** and 1 cup **semisweet chocolate chips;** cook over low heat, stirring, until chocolate is melted (about 3 minutes). Stir in 1 teaspoon **vanilla** (or 2 tablespoons mint-flavored liqueur or rum). Serve warm; or let cool, then cover and refrigerate for up to 3 days. Warm over low heat before serving. Makes ¾ cup.

Per tablespoon: 95 calories, 1 g protein, 9 g carbohydrates, 6 g total fat, 7 mg cholesterol, 2 mg sodium

Raspberry or Strawberry Sauce

Thaw 1 package (10 oz.) **frozen sweetened raspberries** or strawberries. In a 1½- to 2-quart pan, combine thawed berries and their juice; ½ teaspoon

cornstarch; and 1 tablespoon **light corn syrup.** Stir until cornstarch is dissolved; then bring to a boil over medium-high heat, stirring often. Continue to boil, stirring constantly, until sauce is slightly thickened (about 2 more minutes). Let cool; cover and refrigerate until cold. Serve, or store in refrigerator for up to 2 days. Makes about 1 cup.

Per tablespoon: 22 calories, 0.1 g protein, 6 g carbohydrates, 0 g total fat, 0 mg cholesterol, 2 mg sodium

Cherry-Maple Syrup

In a 1-quart pan, combine 6 tablespoons *each* **maple syrup** and **cherry preserves.** Cook over medium heat, stirring, until smoothly blended and hot (3 to 5 minutes). Serve warm. Makes ¾ cup.

Per tablespoon: 52 calories, 0.1 g protein, 13 g carbohydrates, 0 g total fat, 0 mg cholesterol, 2 mg sodium

Spiced Apple Syrup

In a 1-quart pan, combine ¼ cup **apple butter** and ½ cup **maple syrup.** Cook over medium heat, stirring, until smoothly blended and hot (3 to 5 minutes). Serve warm. Makes ¾ cup.

Per tablespoon: 44 calories, 0 g protein, 11 g carbohydrates, 0 g total fat, 0 mg cholesterol, 1 mg sodium

Spiced Rum Syrup

In a 1-quart pan, combine ¼ cup **sugar,** ¾ cup **water,** and 1 teaspoon **whole cloves.** Bring to a boil over high heat; reduce heat and simmer until reduced to about ½ cup (about 5 minutes). Remove from heat and stir in 1 tablespoon **rum.** Let cool. Serve, or cover and refrigerate for up to 5 days. Makes about ½ cup.

Per tablespoon: 29 calories, 0 g protein, 6 g carbohydrates, 0.1 g total fat, 0 mg cholesterol, 0.7 mg sodium

Wine-glazed Baked Pears

Preparation time: About 5 minutes

Baking time: 1 to 1¼ hours

This dessert's succulent flavors bely its ease of preparation: you simply bake whole pears in red wine until browned and tender. Offer as a fitting conclusion to a pasta dinner, accompanied by purchased amaretto-flavored cookies.

- 2   medium-size firm-ripe Bosc or Comice pears
- ½   cup dry red wine
- 3   tablespoons sugar
- ¼   cup water
     Amaretto-flavored cookies

If necessary, trim bases of pears so fruit will stand upright. Set pears side by side in a shallow baking dish or pan (they should fit snugly). Pour wine over pears; sprinkle with 2 tablespoons of the sugar.

Bake in a 425° oven for 45 minutes. Mix water and remaining 1 tablespoon sugar into pan juices; baste pears well with mixture. Continue to bake, basting occasionally with pan juices, until pears are richly browned and tender when pierced (15 to 30 more minutes). Serve pears warm or at room temperature.

To serve, place pears on 2 dessert plates; spoon pan juices over fruit and offer cookies alongside. Makes 2 servings.

Per serving: 175 calories, 0.8 g protein, 45 g carbohydrates, 0.7 g total fat, 0 mg cholesterol, 3 mg sodium

Crunch-top Baked Apples

Preparation time: About 10 minutes

Baking time: About 30 minutes

What's the ideal dessert for a homestyle menu? After a tender pot roast or hearty beef stew, nothing tastes better than these plump, granola-stuffed baked apples. Serve them warm from the oven or at room temperature, perhaps with a splash of cream.

- 2   Golden Delicious, Winesap, or McIntosh apples, *each* about 3 inches in diameter
- ½   cup granola cereal
- 2   tablespoons butter or margarine, at room temperature
- 2   tablespoons firmly packed brown sugar
- ½   cup apple juice
     Whipping cream or half-and-half (optional)

Core apples, using an apple corer. Mix granola, butter, and sugar; then press half the mixture into center of each apple, mounding any excess on top.

Set apples slightly apart in a small, shallow baking dish. Pour apple juice into dish.

Bake in a 350° oven until apples are tender when pierced (about 30 minutes). Serve warm or at room temperature.

To serve, spoon apples and cooking juices into 2 dessert bowls. Offer cream to pour over apples, if desired. Makes 2 servings.

Per serving: 420 calories, 4 g protein, 65 g carbohydrates, 18 g total fat, 31 mg cholesterol, 135 mg sodium

Double Peanut Brittle Sundaes

Preparation time: About 10 minutes

Treat yourselves like kids again—indulge in an ice cream delight. Chopped peanuts plus peanut brittle give these sundaes a double crunch. (They are filling, so serve them after a light meal of soup and salad.)

> **4** ounces peanut brittle
> **¼** cup salted roasted peanuts, coarsely chopped
> **⅓** cup purchased caramel sauce
> **About 1 pint rich vanilla ice cream**
> **Whipped cream (optional)**

Break off and set aside 2 large (2½-inch-wide) chunks of peanut brittle. Coarsely crush remaining brittle.

In each of 2 deep dessert dishes or goblets (at least 12-oz. size), layer one-third each of the crushed brittle, peanuts, and caramel sauce. Place a big scoop of ice cream in each dish. Repeat layers; then top sundaes equally with remaining crushed brittle, peanuts, and caramel sauce.

Garnish each sundae with a mound of whipped cream, if desired; then stick a chunk of reserved brittle into ice cream. Serve at once. Makes 2 servings.

Per serving: 797 calories, 14 g protein, 125 g carbohydrates, 29 g total fat, 60 mg cholesterol, 212 mg sodium

Coffee Banana Rum Slush

Preparation time: About 15 minutes

Freezing time: At least 2 hours

After-dinner drink or dessert? This blend of frosty-cold coffee, frozen bananas, milk, and a splash of rum fills both roles at once. It's a good finale to a summertime meal such as Grilled Chicken & Vegetables with Sesame Sauce (page 46).

> **2** small ripe bananas
> **Double-strength Coffee (recipe follows)**
> **1** cup milk
> **2** to 3 tablespoons firmly packed brown sugar
> **2** to 5 tablespoons rum (optional)
> **Ground cinnamon**

Peel bananas, then cut into about ½-inch-thick slices. Place slices slightly apart in an 8- or 9-inch baking pan. Cover and freeze until bananas are frozen (at least 2 hours) or for up to 1 week. Meanwhile, prepare Double-strength Coffee; cover and refrigerate until cold (at least 30 minutes).

In a blender or food processor, combine frozen banana slices, coffee, and milk. Whirl until puréed; add sugar and rum (if used) and whirl again. Pour into 2 chilled glasses and sprinkle with cinnamon. Makes 2 servings.

Double-strength Coffee. Measure ¼ cup finely ground **regular or decaffeinated espresso** or other dark roast coffee into a cone lined with a paper coffee filter. Pour about ¾ cup **hot water** (190° to 195°F) through filter into a glass measure. (Or put coffee into a filter-plunger pot, add water, and let stand for 2 to 3 minutes; then push plunger.)

Per serving: 226 calories, 5 g protein, 44 g carbohydrates, 5 g total fat, 17 mg cholesterol, 69 mg sodium

Sweet dreams come true at the soda fountain—and at home, too. If dessert is your favorite part of the day, you'll go nuts for Double Peanut Brittle Sundaes (recipe on facing page) and Chocolate Chip Peanut Meltaways (recipe on page 80).

79

Chocolate Chip Peanut Meltaways

Preparation time: About 20 minutes

Baking time: 10 to 12 minutes

If you think baking a batch of cookies for two is too much effort, the irresistible flavor of these treats will change your mind. Because the cookies store well, you'll have a sweet on hand for several meals in a row. Of course, you needn't save these rich morsels for dessert; served with hot coffee, they're perfect for a sweet respite on a busy afternoon.

- ½   **cup (¼ lb.) butter or margarine, at room temperature**
- ½   **cup powdered sugar**
- ½   **teaspoon vanilla**
- ⅛   **teaspoon almond extract**
- 1   **cup all-purpose flour**
- ⅓   **cup chopped salted roasted peanuts**
- ¼   **cup finely chopped semisweet chocolate**
- 1   **tablespoon unsweetened cocoa**

In a medium-size bowl, beat together butter and ¼ cup of the sugar until creamy. Beat in vanilla and almond extract. Add flour; mix until dough is well blended and holds together. Then blend in peanuts and chocolate.

Roll dough into 1-inch balls; place about 1½ inches apart on an ungreased 12- by 15-inch baking sheet. Bake in a 375° oven until cookies are pale gold (10 to 12 minutes). Let cool briefly.

Meanwhile, mix remaining ¼ cup sugar and cocoa in a small bowl. Carefully roll cookies, a few at a time, in cocoa mixture to coat. Let cool completely on racks. Serve, or store airtight for up to 5 days. Makes about 20 cookies.

Per cookie: 101 calories, 1 g protein, 10 g carbohydrates, 7 g total fat, 12 mg cholesterol, 57 mg sodium

Oat Shortbread Hearts

Preparation time: About 15 minutes

Baking time: About 40 minutes

Cooling time: About 15 minutes

For those who prefer less-sweet desserts, present these heart-shaped shortbreads with cherry preserves and gouda cheese. Made with nutritious whole wheat flour and rolled oats, the crunchy cookies nicely round off a wholesome main course such as Fresh Ravioli & Cabbage Soup (page 19).

- ¼   **cup butter or margarine, at room temperature**
- 2   **tablespoons sugar**
- ½   **cup whole wheat flour**
- ¼   **cup regular rolled oats**
      Cherry preserves
      Gouda or sharp Cheddar cheese

In a medium-size bowl, beat butter and sugar until creamy. Add flour and oats; mix until incorporated. (Or combine butter, sugar, and flour in a food processor and whirl until combined; then add oats and stir until dough holds together.)

Firmly pat dough into 4 or 5 ungreased heart-shaped cookie molds, each about 2½ inches in diameter. Place on a baking sheet. (Or, on a greased baking sheet, pat dough into a circle about 5 inches in diameter.) Bake in a 325° oven until shortbread is deep golden (about 40 minutes). If shortbread is not in molds, cut it into 4 or 5 equal pieces with a knife.

Let shortbread cool in molds (or on baking sheet) on a rack for about 15 minutes. Loosen edges of cookies in molds with tip of a knife, then invert cookies onto a plate. (Or lift pieces from baking sheet and place on plate.) Serve warm or cool, with preserves and cheese to add to taste. Makes 2 servings.

Per serving: 392 calories, 6 g protein, 41 g carbohydrates, 24 g total fat, 62 mg cholesterol, 236 mg sodium

Orange Polenta Cakes

Preparation time: About 15 minutes

Cooking time: About 11 minutes

Cooling time: At least 5 minutes

Polenta—coarsely ground cornmeal—is cooked in orange juice, lightly sweetened with honey, and pressed into molds for a quick, easy, and wholesome confection. Serve after a light Italian-style lunch of cold sliced cheeses, prosciutto, marinated vegetables, and crusty bread.

¼	teaspoon grated orange peel
1¼	cups orange juice
¼	teaspoon salt (optional)
½	cup polenta or yellow cornmeal
1	tablespoon butter or margarine
2	tablespoons honey
2	tablespoons sweetened shredded coconut
½	cup plain lowfat yogurt
	Honey
	About 1 cup peeled, sliced fresh fruit (such as kiwi fruit, oranges, or bananas)

In a 1½- to 2-quart pan, combine orange peel, orange juice, and salt (if used). Bring to a boil over high heat. Gradually add polenta, stirring until blended. Reduce heat to medium and cook, stirring with a long-handled spoon, until polenta is thick (about 1 minute); watch for splatters. Reduce heat to low; continue to stir until polenta stops flowing after spoon is drawn across pan bottom (about 5 more minutes). Stir in butter and the 2 tablespoons honey.

Spoon half the polenta mixture into each of 2 buttered 6-ounce custard cups or decorative molds. Press polenta solidly into cups. Let cool for at least 5 minutes or up to 30 minutes, then run a knife around edges of molds and invert polenta onto 2 dessert plates.

Toast coconut in a small frying pan over medium heat until golden (about 5 minutes), stirring often. Sprinkle coconut over polenta cakes. Sweeten yogurt to taste with honey; offer yogurt and fruit to spoon over each serving. Makes 2 servings.

Per serving: 420 calories, 8 g protein, 80 g carbohydrates, 9 g total fat, 19 mg cholesterol, 118 mg sodium

Tortilla Turtles

Preparation time: About 10 minutes

Cooking time: About 7 minutes

If you're looking for a special coffeetime treat or a finishing touch to a Mexican-style meal, you'll be delighted with these crunchy baked tortillas—first sprinkled with cinnamon and sugar, then drizzled with a creamy chocolate-caramel sauce. (The sauce is an excellent topping for ice cream, too.)

2	flour tortillas, *each* about 7 inches in diameter
	Salad oil
2	tablespoons sugar
½	teaspoon ground cinnamon
2	ounces caramels (about ⅓ cup), unwrapped
¼	cup semisweet chocolate chips
2	tablespoons whipping cream

Cut tortillas into quarters. In a medium-size frying pan, heat ¼ inch oil over high heat until hot. Add half the tortilla quarters and cook, turning once, until crisp and lightly browned (about 1 minute). Drain on paper towels. Repeat to cook remaining tortilla quarters.

In a paper or plastic bag, mix sugar and cinnamon. Add 2 tortilla quarters and gently shake bag to coat. Place tortillas on a wide plate. Repeat with remaining tortilla quarters.

In a 1-quart pan, combine caramels, chocolate chips, and cream. Cook over medium-low heat, stirring, until mixture is smoothly melted (about 5 minutes). Drizzle about half the sauce over tortillas; serve extra sauce alongside for dipping. Makes 2 servings.

Per serving: 429 calories, 5 g protein, 61 g carbohydrates, 20 g total fat, 17 mg cholesterol, 209 mg sodium

Spend the evening in Paris with this spectacular bistro menu. Romaine Salad with Blue Cheese Toasts (recipe on page 84) starts off a meal of meaty Lamb Chops with Juniper Berries (recipe on page 85), wedges of Crisp Herbed Potato Cake (recipe on page 85), and tender braised escarole. It all adds up to incomparable dining à deux!

Candlelight Classics

Cooking for two means different things at different times. The preceding chapters offer a panoply of recipes for everyday dining. But for those evenings when you want dinner to be more than just another meal, choose one of the five menus we present here. Each provides recipes, tips for preparation and serving, even ideas for china and table linens—everything you need to set the mood for an unforgettable night. All you add is the candlelight and romance.

Take a European holiday with our first menu, a French-inspired bistro feast. Another time, when the weather is chilly and the hearth beckons, snuggle up with a Cozy Crab Supper of hot seafood cakes and comforting soup. To celebrate Valentine's Day, try a heartwarming trio of omelet, salad, and golden popovers. On a soft summer night, head outdoors with our make-ahead Oriental Evening Picnic. And on the most special occasion of all—your anniversary—treat yourselves to a champagne celebration that starts with succulent fresh oysters, stars richly sauced scallops and lobster, and finishes with chocolate truffles.

On red-letter days or whenever you're just in the mood for a private celebration, you'll return time and again to the suggestions in this chapter. The recipes here are bound to become classics in your repertoire of special menus for two.

Bistro Dining à Deux

MENU

Romaine Salad with Blue Cheese Toasts

Lamb Chops with Juniper Berries

Crisp Herbed Potato Cake

Braised Escarole or Swiss Chard

Minted Raspberries with White Chocolate

French Burgundy or California Pinot Noir

France has long inspired notions of love; its cities, vineyards, language, and food all seem imbued with a heady *amour*. Today, through the renaissance of bistro cooking, we're discovering an aspect of French cuisine that's delightfully unpretentious, yet undeniably romantic. Simple food, served in generous proportions, typifies the bistro style. You'll find that these dishes lend themselves naturally to a cozy, intimate setting: a crisp checked tablecloth, creamy white dishes, and stubby tumblers to fill with red wine.

The menu above offers the best of bistro fare. A crunchy salad of romaine lettuce, candied pecans, and pungent blue cheese sets the tone. For the main course, sturdy double-rib lamb chops with a juniper berry–garlic coating are accompanied by a crisp, oven-browned cake of herb-seasoned sliced potatoes. Alongside, offer a simply prepared vegetable; we suggest braised escarole or Swiss chard. Buy about 8 ounces of either green; rinse and coarsely chop the leaves, then cook them, covered, in about 1 inch of boiling water until tender (about 10 minutes). Drain well; stir in some butter, if you like, and season with salt and pepper.

To conclude the meal in a truly French fashion, forgo pastry and cake for dressed-up fresh fruit: ruby-red raspberries drizzled with a minty syrup and showered with grated white chocolate. With the berries, you might also offer a soft ripened cheese such as St. André.

A French Burgundy (such as Morey St. Denis) or California Pinot Noir tastefully complements every course, from salad to dessert.

Pictured on page 82

Romaine Salad with Blue Cheese Toasts

Preparation time: About 15 minutes

Cooking time: About 30 minutes

¼	cup sugar
½	cup pecan halves
2	slices sourdough bread, *each* about 4 by 5 inches
⅓	cup crumbled blue cheese
	Blue Cheese Vinaigrette (recipe follows)
4	cups bite-size pieces romaine lettuce, rinsed and crisped

Place sugar and pecans in a small frying pan. Cook over medium-high heat, stirring often, until sugar is melted and amber in color (about 5 minutes). Spread pecan mixture on a buttered 12-inch square of foil. Let cool, then break pecans apart.

Trim and discard crusts from bread, then cut each slice diagonally into 2 triangles. Place bread on a rack on a baking sheet and bake in a 325° oven until very crisp (about 20 minutes). Lightly press cheese onto toast; continue to bake until cheese is melted (about 5 more minutes). Meanwhile, prepare Blue Cheese Vinaigrette.

In a bowl, mix lettuce and pecans with vinaigrette. Divide salad between 2 plates; top with blue cheese toasts. Makes 2 servings.

Blue Cheese Vinaigrette. In a small bowl, whisk together 2 tablespoons **red wine vinegar** and 3 tablespoons **salad oil**. Stir in ¼ cup crumbled **blue cheese**. Season vinaigrette to taste with freshly ground **pepper**.

Per serving: 697 calories, 15 g protein, 50 g carbohydrates, 51 g total fat, 30 mg cholesterol, 720 mg sodium

Pictured on page 82

Lamb Chops with Juniper Berries

Preparation time: About 10 minutes

Cooking time: 21 to 23 minutes

    Juniper Berry Paste (recipe follows)
2   **double-rib lamb chops (about 6 oz. *each*), trimmed of excess fat**
1   **tablespoon butter or margarine**
¼   cup *each* **chicken broth and dry red wine**
1   **tablespoon minced shallot**

Prepare Juniper Berry Paste. Rub paste evenly over each chop.

Melt 1½ teaspoons of the butter in an 8- to 10-inch frying pan over medium heat. Add chops and cook, turning as needed, until meat is well browned on both sides but still pink in center; cut to test (18 to 20 minutes; pan drippings will be blackened). Transfer chops to 2 warm dinner plates; keep warm.

To pan, add broth, wine, and shallot; bring to a boil over high heat, stirring to scrape up browned bits. Boil until reduced by half (about 3 minutes). Remove from heat, add remaining 1½ teaspoons butter, and stir until melted. Pour sauce over chops. Makes 2 servings.

Juniper Berry Paste. Combine 1 tablespoon crushed **dry juniper berries,** ½ teaspoon coarsely ground **pepper,** and 1 clove **garlic,** minced or pressed.

Per serving: 206 calories, 15 g protein, 2 g carbohydrates, 13 g total fat, 64 mg cholesterol, 237 mg sodium

Pictured on page 82

Crisp Herbed Potato Cake

Preparation time: About 10 minutes

Baking time: About 40 minutes

1   **large russet potato**
2   **tablespoons butter or margarine, melted**
½   **teaspoon *each* dry rosemary and dry thyme**

Peel potato and cut crosswise into even, very thin slices (⅛ inch or thinner). Combine butter, rosemary, and thyme; coat sides and bottom of an 8- or 9-inch glass pie dish with half the butter mixture. Neatly arrange potato slices in concentric circles to form an even layer in dish, overlapping slices to fit. Drizzle remaining butter mixture over potato.

Bake on bottom rack of a 450° oven until potato cake is well browned and crisp on both top and bottom (about 40 minutes). To unmold potato cake, invert a dinner plate over dish; using pot holders to hold plate in place, turn over both dish and plate so cake slides out. Cut into wedges to serve. Makes 2 servings.

Per serving: 195 calories, 2 g protein, 21 g carbohydrates, 12 g total fat, 31 mg cholesterol, 126 mg sodium

Minted Raspberries with White Chocolate

Preparation time: About 5 minutes

Cooking time: About 5 minutes

Cooling time: About 20 minutes

Chilling time: At least 4 hours

    Mint Syrup (recipe follows)
2   **cups raspberries**
1   **ounce white chocolate, finely grated**

Prepare, cool, and chill Mint Syrup.

To serve, divide raspberries between 2 dessert dishes or goblets; drizzle each serving with half the Mint Syrup. Sprinkle evenly with chocolate. Makes 2 servings.

Mint Syrup. In a 1- to 2-quart pan, stir together 1 cup **water** and ½ cup **sugar.** Bring to a boil over high heat. Stir in ½ cup firmly packed **fresh mint leaves,** return to a boil, and boil until reduced by half (about 5 minutes). Remove from heat and let stand until cooled to room temperature (about 20 minutes). Pour syrup through a strainer; discard mint leaves. Cover syrup and refrigerate for at least 4 hours.

Per serving: 334 calories, 2 g protein, 74 g carbohydrates, 5 g total fat, 2 mg cholesterol, 12 mg sodium

Cozy Crab Supper

MENU

Winter Vegetable Soup

Mesclun Salad & Crisp Breadsticks

Crab Cakes with Tomato Chutney

Sliced Oranges & Gingersnaps

Sparkling Cider or Sparkling White Wine

When the bone-chilling winter winds swirl about the house, nothing seems more welcoming than dinner for two by the fire. Fend off the cold with a pair of warming dishes—chunky vegetable soup and savory crab cakes—then round out the meal with no-cook extras, such as a salad of premixed greens (sometimes called mesclun mix), purchased breadsticks, fresh fruit, and crisp cookies.

To get a head start on this no-fuss menu, you can rinse and crisp the greens and shape the crab cakes up to 2 hours in advance. The soup takes only 40 minutes to prepare and cook; just before serving, fry the crab cakes and toss the salad (for vinaigrette ideas, see page 44). Top the crab cakes with your favorite homemade or purchased tomato chutney—then fill your glasses, pull your dinner trays up to the hearth, and toast your cleverness at beating the winter chill so easily!

Pictured on facing page

Winter Vegetable Soup

Preparation time: About 15 minutes

Cooking time: About 23 minutes

8	ounces banana squash
2½	cups chicken broth
1	piece fresh ginger (about 1 by 1½ inches), peeled and cut into matchstick-size pieces
1	cup firmly packed stemmed, slivered mustard greens, rinsed and drained
1	cup chopped cauliflower
½	cup cooked rice

Cut off and discard peel from squash. Cut squash into ½-inch cubes, place in a 2- to 3-quart pan, and add broth and ginger. Bring to a boil over high heat; reduce heat, cover, and simmer until squash is tender when pierced (about 10 minutes).

Add mustard greens and cauliflower to soup, then increase heat to high and bring soup to a boil. Reduce heat, cover, and simmer until cauliflower is tender when pierced (about 10 minutes). Stir in rice and continue to simmer, uncovered, until hot (about 3 more minutes). Makes 2 servings.

Per serving: 161 calories, 8 g protein, 29 g carbohydrates, 2 g total fat, 0 mg cholesterol, 1,255 mg sodium

Pictured on facing page

Crab Cakes with Tomato Chutney

Preparation time: About 15 minutes

Cooking time: About 30 minutes

2	tablespoons butter or margarine
1	small yellow onion, chopped
⅓	pound cooked crabmeat
½	cup fine dry bread crumbs
¼	cup thinly sliced green onions
1	egg, lightly beaten
¼	cup nonfat or lowfat milk
	Tomato or other fruit chutney

Melt 2 teaspoons of the butter in a wide nonstick frying pan over medium heat. Add yellow onion and cook, stirring often, until lightly browned and very soft (about 20 minutes).

Scrape cooked onion into a bowl and add crab, crumbs, green onions, egg, and milk; mix well. Divide mixture into 6 equal portions and shape each into a 3-inch-diameter patty. (At this point, you may place patties on a plate in a single layer, cover, and refrigerate for up to 2 hours.)

Melt remaining 4 teaspoons butter in same frying pan over medium-high heat. Add crab cakes in a single layer (do not crowd pan); cook until bottoms are lightly browned (about 5 minutes). With a wide spatula, carefully turn cakes over and cook until browned on other side (about 5 more minutes). Transfer to a plate and keep warm.

To serve, arrange 3 crab cakes on each of 2 dinner plates. Offer chutney to add to taste. Makes 2 servings.

Per serving: 334 calories, 23 g protein, 22 g carbohydrates, 17 g total fat, 214 mg cholesterol, 558 mg sodium

Pull your trays up to the fireplace, uncork a bottle of sparkling cider,
and relax together with this simple menu: chunky Winter Vegetable Soup
(recipe on facing page), Crab Cakes with Tomato Chutney (recipe on facing
page), tossed field greens with oil and vinegar, and crisp breadsticks.
There's no better way to unwind on a chilly evening.

Anniversary Champagne Celebration

MENU

Oysters Mignonette

Scallops & Lobster in Tomato Cream Sauce

Steamed Asparagus & Baby Squash

Petite Dinner Rolls with Butter Flowers

Chocolate Hearts

Champagne

Beautiful to look at and luxurious to eat, this menu is the epitome of elegant dining *à deux*—and the ideal choice for the most significant of occasions. An anniversary, whether first, fifth, or fiftieth, provides our favorite reason to pull out all the stops and offer this spectacular meal—but birthdays, promotions, and Valentine's Day offer equally good excuses!

Set a lovely, intimate table with your finest china, crystal, and linen; for the centerpiece, choose a soft bouquet of roses, tulips, or peonies. Begin the feast with raw oysters on the half shell to dip in a peppery shallot sauce, then go on to the main course: rich lobster and delicate scallops in velvety tomato cream. (By using lobster tails rather than the whole shellfish, you can enjoy this favorite seafood with very little waste.) To complement the entrée, arrange steamed asparagus spears and baby summer squash on each plate; you'll need about ⅓ pound of each vegetable. For the bread, search out petite, flaky dinner rolls at your favorite bakery. Make the butter special, too: slice thin slabs from a chilled stick, then cut out flowers or other designs using petit four cutters (available in most cookware shops).

Finally, to melt your loved one's heart, conclude the celebration with handmade chocolate truffles—in heart shapes, of course. You may want to offer espresso with the truffles, but we feel that bubbly champagne beautifully accompanies the entire meal. Cheers!

Oysters Mignonette

Preparation time: About 20 minutes

12	raw oysters in the shell
3	tablespoons white wine vinegar
1	tablespoon water
2	teaspoons minced shallot
¼	teaspoon coarsely ground pepper

Scrub oysters under cold running water with a stiff brush. Then firmly hold each oyster, cup side down, in a towel; work tip of an oyster knife between shells near hinge (look for a small opening). With a twist of the wrist, turn knife sideways to pop open shell. Slide knife along inside top shell to sever the muscle connecting meat and shell; discard top shell. Slide knife under oyster to loosen it from bottom shell. Wipe off any fragments of shell.

Place oysters on a bed of crushed ice or rock salt in a shallow dish. In a small (about ¼-cup) bowl, stir together vinegar, water, shallot, and pepper. Place bowl of sauce in center of dish with oysters surrounding it. To eat, spear an oyster with a small fork and dip into sauce. Makes 2 servings.

Per serving: 65 calories, 6 g protein, 5 g carbohydrates, 2 g total fat, 47 mg cholesterol, 96 mg sodium

Scallops & Lobster in Tomato Cream Sauce

Preparation time: About 15 minutes

Cooking time: About 35 minutes

1	lobster tail (6 to 8 oz.), thawed if frozen
2	tablespoons olive oil
1	small onion, finely chopped
1	cup peeled, seeded, chopped tomatoes
⅓	cup whipping cream
2	tablespoons dry vermouth
	Salt and pepper
½	cup *each* water and dry white wine
6	whole black peppercorns
6	ounces sea scallops
2	tablespoons snipped chives

In a 4- to 6-quart pan, bring about 2 quarts water to a boil over high heat. Add lobster tail. Reduce heat and simmer, uncovered, until meat is opaque in thickest part; cut to test (about 10 minutes). Drain lobster, immerse in ice water until cool, and drain again. With kitchen scissors, clip fins from sides of soft undershell of lobster tail, then snip along edges. Lift off and discard undershell. Working from body end, carefully remove meat from shell in one piece. Thinly slice meat crosswise; set aside.

Heat oil in a medium-size frying pan over medium heat. Add onion; cook, stirring often, until soft and golden (about 10 minutes). Add tomatoes; bring to a boil over high heat, then reduce heat and simmer until tomatoes are softened (about 5 minutes), stirring occasionally. Add cream and vermouth, increase heat, and bring to a boil. Reduce heat to medium-low and cook, stirring often, until mixture is reduced by half (about 5 minutes); season to taste with salt and pepper. Transfer to a food processor and whirl until puréed. Return sauce to pan and keep warm over very low heat.

In a medium-size frying pan, combine water, wine, and peppercorns. Bring to a boil over high heat, then reduce heat to medium. Rinse and drain scallops, add to pan, and cook until opaque in center; cut to test (about 3 minutes). With a slotted spoon, lift scallops from pan; set aside on a warm plate. Add lobster to liquid in pan; cook just until heated through (about 2 minutes). With a slotted spoon, transfer lobster to plate with scallops.

Divide tomato cream sauce between 2 warm dinner plates; arrange scallops and lobster over sauce. Sprinkle with chives. Makes 2 servings.

Per serving: 443 calories, 27 g protein, 10 g carbohydrates, 27 g total fat, 111 mg cholesterol, 369 mg sodium

Chocolate Hearts

Preparation time: About 5 minutes

Cooking time: About 3 minutes

Freezing time: 45 to 60 minutes

4	ounces semisweet chocolate, finely chopped; or about ⅔ cup semisweet chocolate chips
3	tablespoons whipping cream
1	tablespoon crème de menthe; or ¼ teaspoon mint extract and 1 tablespoon whipping cream
2	tablespoons unsweetened cocoa

In a 1- to 2-quart pan, combine chocolate and cream. Stir over low heat until smoothly melted (about 3 minutes). Remove from heat and stir in crème de menthe.

Line a 4- to 4½-inch-diameter round dish with plastic wrap; pour chocolate mixture into dish. Freeze until firm enough to cut (45 to 60 minutes).

Dust a piece of wax paper with cocoa; lift frozen chocolate from dish and invert onto cocoa-dusted paper. Peel plastic wrap off chocolate. With a 1½- to 2-inch-wide heart-shaped cookie cutter, quickly cut chocolate into 4 hearts. Cut remaining chocolate into bite-size pieces. Turn chocolate hearts and smaller pieces over in cocoa to coat heavily. Cover with plastic wrap and refrigerate until ready to serve. Makes 4 chocolate hearts (plus additional pieces).

Per heart: 188 calories, 2 g protein, 20 g carbohydrates, 13 g total fat, 7 mg cholesterol, 5 mg sodium

Dinner out on the town is a Valentine's Day tradition for many, but home-cooked meals can be just as delicious as fancy restaurant fare—and certainly more intimate. Blue Cheese Omelets, crisp and tart Asparagus Salad, and homey Prosciutto & Fontina Popovers let you save time and money without sacrificing romance. (All three recipes are on the facing page.)

Valentine's Dinner

Valentine's Day dining doesn't have to be lavish. Sometimes the most memorable dinner is a modest meal like this one, cooked and served at home.

Instead of a series of courses, you present three delicious dishes all at once: a blue cheese omelet, a warm asparagus salad, and fragrant popovers. For dessert, relax with a purchased torte. Set the table with pretty placemats and your everyday china; tuck a valentine under each plate. And finally, don't forget to say "I love you."

Pictured on facing page

Blue Cheese Omelets

Preparation time: About 10 minutes

Cooking time: About 8 minutes

4	eggs
2	tablespoons water
2	teaspoons butter or margarine
2	tablespoons crumbled blue cheese
	Salt and pepper

In a bowl, lightly beat eggs and water to blend. Melt 1 teaspoon of the butter in an 8- to 10-inch nonstick frying pan over medium-high heat; tilt pan to coat bottom and sides. Pour in half the egg mixture and cook, lifting edges with a spatula to let uncooked portion flow underneath, until set but still moist on top (about 4 minutes). Sprinkle half the cheese down center of omelet. With a spatula, lift half the omelet and fold over cheese. Shake pan to slide omelet out onto a warm dinner plate; keep

warm. Repeat to cook a second omelet. Season to taste with salt and pepper. Makes 2 servings.

Per serving: 213 calories, 14 g protein, 1 g carbohydrates, 16 g total fat, 442 mg cholesterol, 283 mg sodium

Pictured on facing page

Asparagus Salad

Preparation time: About 10 minutes

Cooking time: About 4 minutes

8	ounces asparagus, tough ends removed
2	tablespoons olive oil
1	tablespoon lemon juice
1	tablespoon finely shredded Parmesan cheese
2	lemon wedges

Cook asparagus in 1 inch of boiling water just until tender-crisp to bite (about 4 minutes). Drain.

Arrange warm asparagus on 2 dinner plates. Mix oil and lemon juice; spoon over asparagus. Sprinkle asparagus with cheese. Garnish each salad with a lemon wedge. Makes 2 servings.

Per serving: 151 calories, 3 g protein, 6 g carbohydrates, 14 g total fat, 2 mg cholesterol, 50 mg sodium

Pictured on facing page

Prosciutto & Fontina Popovers

Preparation time: About 10 minutes

Baking time: About 50 minutes

1	egg
½	cup *each* all-purpose flour and milk
1	ounce prosciutto or cooked ham, chopped
¼	cup shredded fontina cheese
1	tablespoon minced green onion

Heavily butter four 2- to 2½-inch-wide muffin cups or heavy popover cups.

In a blender, whirl egg, flour, and milk until smoothly blended. Stir in prosciutto, cheese, and onion. Immediately pour batter equally into cups. Bake in a 375° oven until popovers are very well browned and firm to the touch (about 50 minutes). Run a knife around edges of popovers to loosen; invert to remove from cups. Makes 4 popovers.

Per popover: 135 calories, 8 g protein, 14 g carbohydrates, 5 g total fat, 70 mg cholesterol, 240 mg sodium

Oriental Evening Picnic

```
MENU
Mustard Shrimp
Chilled Lemon Noodles
Mixed Salad Greens
Strawberries with Gingered Vanilla Yogurt
Giant Fortune Cookies or Almond Cookies
Juice Spritzers
```

Warm evenings invite picnicking. This fully portable menu lets you go wherever you want—you can stay home in your own garden or head to a far-off spot with a special view.

The centerpiece recipe is a salad of crisp greens and cold noodles topped with mustardy shrimp. Pack each element separately; to serve, place the greens on dinner plates, then spoon on the noodles and shrimp. For dessert, offer chilled ripe strawberries with a ginger-seasoned yogurt dip alongside. Bring along some cookies, too; we suggest homemade oversized fortune cookies, each holding a personalized message (make up your own fortunes, or consult a book of poetry for ideas). The cookies are shaped hot from the oven; when you fold them, wear light cotton gloves to protect your hands. If you don't have the time to make cookies, substitute purchased fortune cookies or Chinese almond cookies. Fruity spritzers (with or without alcohol), transported in an attractive sealed jug or pitcher, are just right for sipping.

To get a head start on the menu, bake the cookies and prepare the shrimp and noodles the day before; also wash and crisp about 4 cups of salad greens and stir together the yogurt dip. If you'll be travelling for any distance, pack the containers of food in a refrigerated chest. You'll also need ice for the spritzers—and don't forget a blanket or cloth to cushion your picnic site.

Mustard Shrimp *coquel*

Preparation time: About 15 minutes

Cooking time: About 15 minutes

Chilling time: At least 1 hour

2	tablespoons butter or salad oil
2	cloves garlic, minced or pressed
¼	cup finely chopped onion
⅛	teaspoon ground red pepper (cayenne)
8 – 12	ounces large raw shrimp, shelled and deveined
¼	cup *each* dry sherry and white wine vinegar
1	tablespoon Dijon mustard
1	tablespoon finely chopped fresh tarragon or 1 teaspoon dry tarragon

(handwritten: 1 by first 2; 8 by the shrimp line; 3 tbsp by the sherry/vinegar line)

Melt butter in a wide frying pan over medium-high heat. Add garlic, onion, and red pepper; cook, stirring often, until onion is soft and golden (about 10 minutes). Add shrimp and cook, stirring, until just opaque in center; cut to test (about 5 minutes). Add sherry, vinegar, mustard, and tarragon; bring to a boil, stirring. Remove from heat and let cool. Place shrimp mixture in a portable container, cover, and refrigerate for at least 1 hour or until next day. Makes 2 servings.

Per serving: 321 calories, 29 g protein, 10 g carbohydrates, 14 g total fat, 240 mg cholesterol, 550 mg sodium

Chilled Lemon Noodles

Preparation time: About 10 minutes

Cooking time: About 10 minutes

6	ounces dry buckwheat noodles (*soba*) or whole wheat spaghetti
	Lemon Dressing (recipe on facing page)

In a 5- to 6-quart pan, cook noodles in about 3 quarts boiling water until just tender to bite (about 10 minutes). Drain, rinse with cold water until cool, and drain again. Set aside.

Prepare Lemon Dressing. Place noodles and dressing in a portable container and toss well;

cover and refrigerate until ready to serve or until next day. Makes 2 servings.

Lemon Dressing. In a small bowl, stir together ¼ cup **lemon juice**, 2 tablespoons **soy sauce**, 2 teaspoons *each* **Oriental sesame oil** and finely chopped **fresh ginger**, and 1 teaspoon **sugar**.

Per serving: 351 calories, 13 g protein, 69 g carbohydrates, 5 g total fat, 0 mg cholesterol, 1,709 mg sodium

Strawberries with Gingered Vanilla Yogurt

Preparation time: About 10 minutes

- ¾ cup vanilla-flavored lowfat yogurt
- ¼ teaspoon ground ginger
- 2 cups large strawberries, hulled

In a small portable container, stir together yogurt and ginger. Pack strawberries in a separate container. To serve, offer yogurt mixture as a dip alongside strawberries. Makes 2 servings.

Per serving: 119 calories, 5 g protein, 23 g carbohydrates, 2 g total fat, 4 mg cholesterol, 58 mg sodium

Juice Spritzers

Preparation time: About 10 minutes

- 2 cups white grape juice, cranberry juice, or guava juice
- 1 cup sparkling water or sparkling dry white wine, such as Asti Spumante or champagne
  Ice cubes
  Lemon or lime slices
- ⅓ cup raspberries or bite-size pieces cantaloupe, honeydew melon, or peeled peaches (optional)

In a 1-quart sealable jug or pitcher, mix juice and water. To serve, place ice in each of two 12- to 16-ounce glasses; add juice mixture and lemon or lime slices. If desired, float berries or fruit pieces on top of each drink. Makes 2 servings.

Per serving: 160 calories, 0 g protein, 40 g carbohydrates, 0 g total fat, 0 mg cholesterol, 20 mg sodium

Giant Fortune Cookies

Preparation time: About 25 minutes

Baking time: About 1 hour

	Solid vegetable shortening
½	cup all-purpose flour
1	tablespoon cornstarch
¼	cup sugar
¼	teaspoon salt
¼	cup salad oil
¼	cup egg whites
1½	teaspoons water
1	teaspoon vanilla

Type or print fortunes, allowing a 1- by 3-inch area of paper for each. Cut paper into strips, separating individual fortunes; place near oven.

Thoroughly grease a baking sheet with vegetable shortening. In a bowl, stir together flour, cornstarch, sugar, and salt. Add oil and egg whites and beat until smooth; beat in water and vanilla. Bake one cookie at a time: drop a scant ¼ cup of batter onto baking sheet and spread evenly into a 7-inch circle. Bake in a 300° oven until light golden brown (about 14 minutes); if underbaked, cookies will tear during shaping.

To shape cookies, wear trim-fitting cotton gloves. With a wide spatula, remove cookie from baking sheet; flip it over into gloved hand. Hold prepared fortune in center of cookie while you fold cookie in half; work quickly. (If cookie hardens too fast, you can restore its flexibility by returning it to the oven for about a minute.) Bend cookie ends together to form a crescent with open side of cookie on top edge. Hold cookie for a minute or two so it will hold its shape as it cools. Repeat steps to bake remaining batter, using a cold, well-greased baking sheet for each cookie. Store cookies airtight for up to 1 day. Makes 4 cookies.

Per cookie: 245 calories, 3 g protein, 27 g carbohydrates, 14 g total fat, 0 mg cholesterol, 163 mg sodium

Index

*If extravagance is what you're after, sumptuous
Spinach Pasta & Salmon in Champagne Cream Sauce (recipe on page 36)
is the dinner for you. It's worthy of the most festive occcasions,
especially when accompanied by a bottle of bubbly.*

95